WEDDING
CAKES

by
Mary Ford

WITH STEP-BY-STEP INSTRUCTIONS

Printed and bound in Great Britain by Purnell Book Productions Ltd.

ISBN 0 946429 06 5

All cake designs in this book have been previously published in either Mary Ford's 101 Cake Designs or Mary Ford's Cake Designs - Another 101

The Authors.

Mary was born in Wick Village, near Bristol. Her interest in cake icing started when her father, a flour miller, encouraged her to take up the craft.

On leaving school, therefore, Mary went straight into a bakery on a four-year apprenticeship, with a day release each week to attend a course at Bristol Technical College, where she gained her Final City and Guilds in Bread Making and Flour Confectionery.

Having moved to London to gain greater experience, Mary finally settled in Bournemouth where she started teaching cake icing in Bournemouth and Southampton Colleges. That eventually led to private tuition.

She met and married Michael and as their business increased, so ever larger premises were found to accommodate larger classes. Mary, throughout this period, continued icing cakes to order and instructing students who were arriving from all parts of the World.

Mary makes no secret of the fact that cake decoration is the consuming passion of her life. She has won innumerable awards in the craft.

Michael was born in Croydon, Surrey. His ambition to succeed in the culinary arts began at school, where he was the only boy to study cookery. This led to a three-year course in bread making and flour confectionery at Plymouth Technical College. There Michael achieved the Final City and Guilds in the subject.

He then travelled the country to further his practical experience in various hotels, restaurants and bakeries. He visited Bournemouth to work in a bakery and there met and married Mary in 1970.

His ambition to manage his own business came to fruition 12 months later when, with Mary, he created the forerunner to the Mary Ford Cake Artistry Centre.

Michael introduced a number of ideas in order to expand the company, including mail order, correspondence courses throughout the World and the development and manufacture of cake artistry tools.

A natural follow-up to the correspondence courses was the production of books on cake icing artistry for which Michael has been responsible for all the photography.

Preface

Over many years our friends and customers asked us to produce a cake icing book and this we did in 1982. That book 101 Cake Designs - proved to be a best seller and created the demand for a second book. The challenge became irresistible to us and the result was Mary Ford's Cake Designs - Another 101.

By demand, we are now producing this series of titles devoted to specialist types of cakes, selected from our first two books.

We sincerely trust this book, as well as its companion books, will give much pleasure and help to all who use them in the pursuit of excellence in cake icing artistry.

Our thanks go to Stan and Betty Oddy and all who have helped in the preparation of this book.

Michael and Mary

Introduction

The Mary Ford Story is a fairy tale come true. No waving of a magic wand has however brought about the success and quality of product which is associated with the Mary Ford Cake Artistry Centre. Hard work, dedication, perseverence and consistently high standards of product have achieved this.

Michael and Mary Ford manage their enterprise from premises in Southbourne, Bournemouth, England. From this base they bake and sell their own bread and confectionary; ice celebratory cakes to order and give, amongst other things, instruction in cake icing as well as bread, pastry, cake and chocolate making. Demonstrations in the art of cake icing are featured and the Cake Artistry Centre sells, by mail order and over the counter, all manner of cake icing equipment, decorations and raw materials.

All this is a long way from the one small room in an hotel annexe where, in 1971, Mary commenced instructing just six pupils each session. Michael and Mary progressed to their first retail outlet and then moved to their present address. To raise part of the capital they then needed, their home had to be sold - such was the faith in their own ability and urge to succeed.

The quality of the Mary Ford Centre work is a byword to professionals and amateurs alike and this book is the latest in a comprehensive list of outstanding goods to come from Mary Ford and, as is only to be expected, is produced in a highly professional and, thus, easy to follow manner.

For years now the British have led the world in cake icing artistry - especially in the use of royal icing - and our pre-eminence in this field is due solely to the skills of craftspeople like England's Mary Ford. She is an undoubted world leader in her chosen profession and, through her books on step-by-step icing instructions, has received a well earned international recognition and reputation.

To answer a growing demand for cake icing books on different subjects Mary has specially selected twenty-seven Wedding cake designs from her two best selling books:

Mary Ford 101 Cake Designs

Mary Ford's Cake Designs - Another 101

Without fear of contradiction, it can be said that this beautifully produced book - containing almost 1000 coloured photographs - is a work of art in its own right. For, each of the twenty-seven cake designs featured in the book, enjoys a full-page colour photograph and every stage of each design is pictured in thirty-two step-by-step coloured photographs and supported by easy to follow written instructions.

Other books in the series:

Novelty Cakes
Decorated Cakes
Birthday Cakes

These are outstanding books which both professional and amateur will value owning.

S & B

Contents

Reference table to cake designs.

NAME	STYLE	PAGES	FRUIT CAKE SIZES (inches)	BOARD SIZES (inches	MARZIPAN (lbs)	ROYAL ICING (lbs)	SUGAR PASTE (lbs)
ADELINE	1 tier square	18-20	9	12	2½	3	-
AMELIA	3 tier round	90-92	12, 9, 6	15, 12, 9	6½	7½	-
ANNE	3 tier round	66-68	12, 9, 6	15, 12, 9	6½	7	1
CARMEN	2 tier round	48-50	10, 7	13, 10	3½	4½	-
DAISY	2 tier square	36-38	9, 6	12, 9	3½	4	-
DAWN	3 tier round	57-59	10, 7, 5	14, 10, 7	4	4	-
DENISE	4 tier round	81-83	10, 8, 6, 4	14, 11, 9, 7	5½	6	-
DULCIE	3 tier hexagonal	78-80	12, 10, 8	15, 12, 10	8	9	-
FRANCES	3 tier round	84-86	10, 7, 4	14, 10, 7	4	5	-
GEORGINA	1 tier round	30-32	10	14	2½	3	-
GILLIAN	2 tier square	21-23	11, 7	14, 11	5½	5½	-
GRETA	2 tier heart	42-44	9, 6	13, 9	3	3	-
HEATHER	3 tier square	72-74	10, 8, 6	13, 11, 9	6	6	-
JOY	4 tier square	87-89	12, 10, 8, 6,	16, 13, 11, 9	10	10	-
LAVINIA	3 tier square	63-65	10, 8, 6	14, 10, 8	6	7	-
LISA	3 tier round	60-62	11, 8, 5	14, 11, 8	5	5	-
LIVIA	3 tier heart	69-71	10, 7, 5	14, 10, 8	4	4	-
LUCILLE	3 tier horseshoe	54-56	10, 8, 6	14, 11, 9	4½	7	-
PATRICIA	3 tier square	39-41	12, 9, 6	15, 12, 9	7½	8	-
PETAL	2 tier round	27-29	10, 7	13, 10	3½	4	¼
PRIMROSE	1 tier heart	24-26	12	16	3½	4	-
RENITA	2 tier round	15-17	9, 6	13, 9	3	3	¼
ROSEMARIE	4 tier round	75-77	11, 9, 7, 5	15, 12, 10, 8	6½	7	2
SHARON	2 tier square	33-35	9, 6	13, 9	3½	4½	-
TERESA	4 tier horseshoe	93-95	12, 10, 8, 6	16, 13, 11, 9	7½	9	-
VANESSA	3 tier hexagonal	45-47	12*, 9*, 6*	15, 12, 9	6½	7½	-
WEDGWOOD	3 tier round	51-53	12, 9, 6	15, 12, 9	6½	7	-

* Requires double quantity of cake in tin.
This reference table is a guide to the materials used to produce the actual cakes featured in this book. You can, of course, choose whatever material quantities and sizes you wish. Refer to the main photograph in each instance for the appropriate shape of board and cake.
N.B. STRONGER COLOURS HAVE BEEN USED IN THE PREPARATION OF THE STEP-BY-STEP PHOTOGRAPHS IN THIS BOOK TO ACHIEVE CLARITY OF DEFINITION. NATURALLY, ANY COLOUR CHOICE IS YOURS.

Basic Cake Recipe

Imperial/Metric	American
2 oz/57 g plain flour	½ cup all purpose flour
2 oz/57 g brown sugar	⅓ cup brown sugar
2 oz/57 g butter	¼ cup butter
2½ oz/71 g currants	½ cup currants
2½ oz/71 g sultanas	½ cup seedless white raisins
1 oz/28 g seedless raisins	3 tablespoons seedless raisins
1 oz/28 g glacé cherries	3 tablespoons candied cherries
1½ oz/42 g mixed peel	4½ tablespoons candied peel
¾ oz/21 g ground almonds	2½ tablespoons ground almonds
½ fluid oz/2 teaspoons brandy or rum	2 teaspoons brandy or rum
1 large egg	1 large egg
pinch nutmeg	pinch nutmeg
pinch mixed spice	pinch apple pie spice
pinch salt	pinch salt
¼ lemon zest and juice	¼ lemon zest and juice

Preparation. First line your tin with a double layer of buttered greaseproof paper. Then clean and prepare the fruit, halve the cherries. Mix all fruit together with lemon zest. Sift flour, spices and salt.
Method. Beat the butter until light. Add sugar to butter and beat again until light. Gradually add egg, beating in thoroughly after each addition. Stir in ground almonds. Fold in flour and spices. Finally add fruit together with brandy or rum and lemon juice. Mix well together and transfer to tin.

It is most important to follow the exact measurements and mixture of the foregoing ingredients.

In baking the cake initially, if one pint of water is placed in a meat tray in the bottom of the oven, this will create sufficient humidity to keep the top of the cake moist and ensure level results in baking. Remove water after half baking time.

When the cake is baked, leave it in the tin (pan) for one day, remove from tin (pan) then sprinkle the appropriate quantity of soaking mixture. Wrap cake in waxed paper and leave in a cupboard for three weeks. When the waxed paper becomes sticky, this means that moisture is seeping out, a sure sign that the cake is mature. If more liquid is required, add just before marzipanning. A cake needs no more than three weeks to mature.

CAKE PORTIONS: TO CALCULATE SIZE OF FRUIT CAKE REQUIRED 8 PORTIONS ARE GENERALLY CUT FROM EACH 1 LB OF FINISHED ICED CAKE.
Soaking mixture. Equal quantities of Rum, Sherry and Glycerine or spirits of choice. 1 tbls. per 1 lb of cake when required.

Glycerine – Table for use

For soft-cutting icing (per 1 lb or 454 g or 3½ cups of ready-made Royal Icing) use 1 teaspoon of glycerine for the bottom tier of a 3-tier wedding cake.
2 teaspoons of glycerine for the middle tier.
3 teaspoons of glycerine for the top tier, or for single tier cakes.
(N.B. Glycerine only to be added after Royal Icing has been made.)
NO GLYCERINE IN ROYAL ICING FOR RUNOUTS OR No. 1 WORK.

Royal Icing Recipe

Imperial/Metric
1½ ozs/42 g powdered egg white
½ pint/284 ml cold water
3½ lb/1½ kg best icing sugar sieved
OR
½ oz/14 g powdered egg white
3 fluid ozs/3 tablespoons cold water
1 lb/454 g best icing sugar, sieved
OR
3 egg whites (separated the day before)
1 lb/454 g best icing sugar (approximately) sieved

American
¼ cup powdered egg white + 2 tablespoons
1¼ cups cold water
3½ cups confectioner's sugar sifted
OR
¼ cup powdered egg white
3 tablespoons cold water
3½ cups confectioner's sugar, sifted
OR
3 egg whites (separated the day before)
3½ cups confectioner's sugar (approximately) sifted

Preparation. All equipment used must be perfectly cleaned and sterilised. Pour water into a jug and stir in powdered egg white. This will go lumpy and necessitates standing the mixture for one hour, stirring occasionally. Then strain through a muslin.

Method. Pour solution or egg whites into a mixing bowl and place the icing sugar on top. A drop of blue colour (color) may be added for white icing. Beat on slow speed for appoximately 15-20 minutes or until the right consistency is obtained. (If powdered egg white is used the Royal Icing will keep in good condition for 2 weeks. Fresh egg whites will deteriorate quicker). Store Royal Icing in sealed container in a cool place.

Buttercream
(Referred to as CREAM in the Book)

Imperial/Metric
4 ozs/113 g butter
6-8 ozs/170-227 g icing sugar
1-2 tablespoons warm water
essence or flavouring of choice

American
½ cup butter
1⅓-2 cups confectioner's sugar
1-2 tablespoons warm water
extract or flavouring of choice

Method. Sift icing sugar. Soften butter and beat until light. Gradually add the icing sugar beating well after each addition. Add essence (extract) or flavouring (flavoring) of choice and water (carefully).

Heavy Genoese Sponge Recipe

Imperial/Metric
3 oz/85 g butter
3 oz/85 g margarine
6 oz/170 g caster sugar
3 eggs, lightly beaten
6 oz/170 g self-raising flour sieved

American
6 tablespoons butter
6 tablespoons margarine
¾ cup sugar
3 eggs, lightly beaten
1½ cups self-raising flour sifted

Preparation. First line your tin (pans) with greased greaseproof paper.

Method. Cream butter and margarine. Add sugar and beat until light in colour and fluffy in texture. Add the egg a little at a time beating after each addition. Carefully fold in the flour.
Bake: 190°C, 375°F, Gas 5. 20-25 minutes.

½ recipe makes 1 @ 8″ Rd sponge
or 1 @ 7″ Sq
1 recipe makes 1 @ 10″ Rd sponge
or 1 @ 9″ Sq
1½ recipe makes 1 @ 12″ Rd sponge
or 1 @ 11″ Sq

Sugar Paste Recipe (Cold Fondant Recipe)

Imperial/Metric
1 lb/454 g icing sugar, sieved
1 egg white
2 ozs/57 g liquid glucose
(Slightly warmed)

American
3½ cups Confectioner's sugar, sifted
1 egg white
4 tablespoons liquid glucose
(Slightly warmed)

Method. Add egg white and glucose to icing sugar. Blend all ingredients together. Knead well until a smooth paste is obtained.
Keep in a polythene bag or sealed container and in a cool place. Colour and flavour (flavor) as required.

CONVERSION TABLES

WEIGHT		SIZE	
IMPERIAL	METRIC	IMPERIAL	METRIC
½ oz	14 g	5 ins	12.5 cm
1 oz	28 g	6 ins	15 cm
2 oz	57 g	7 ins	18 cm
3 oz	85 g	8 ins	20.5 cm
4 oz	113 g	9 ins	23 cm
5 oz	142 g	10 ins	25.5 cm
6 oz	170 g	11 ins	28 cm
7 oz	198 g	12 ins	30.5 cm
8 oz	227 g	13 ins	33 cm
9 oz	255 g	14 ins	35.5 cm
10 oz	284 g	15 ins	38 cm
11 oz	312 g	16 ins	40.5 cm
12 oz	340 g		
13 oz	369 g		
14 oz	397 g		
15 oz	425 g		
16 oz	454 g		

	LIQUID	
IMPERIAL	METRIC	AMERICAN
1 tsp.	5 ml	1 tsp
1 tbsp	15 ml	1 tbsp
1 fl.oz	28 ml	⅛ cup
2 fl. oz	57 ml	¼ cup
3 fl. oz	85 ml	⅜ cup
4 fl. oz	113 ml	½ cup
¼ pint	142 ml	⅝ cup
½ pint	284 ml	1¼ cup
1 pint	568 ml	2½ cup

Note: AUSTRALIAN TABLESPOON
4 tsp. 20ml 1 tbsp (AUS)

CAKE SIZES AND QUANTITIES WITH APPROXIMATE BAKING TIMES
(QUANTITIES ARE STATED IN MULTIPLES OF EACH OF THE BASIC RECIPES)

	Basic Fruit Cake Recipe (Bake at 275°F, 140°C, Gas Mark 1)						Heavy Genoese Sponge Recipe (Bake at 375°F, 190°C, Gas Mark 5)		
SIZE ins	ROUND	SQUARE	HORSE SHOE	HEART	HEXAGONAL	APPROX TIMING	ROUND	SQUARE	APPROX TIMING
5	1	1½	-	1½	1	1½-1¾ hrs	-	-	-
6	1½	2	1¼	2	1½	1¾-2 hrs	-	-	-
7	2	3	-	3	2	2½-3 hrs	-	½	20-25 mins
8	3	4	2½	4	3	3½-4 hrs	½	-	20-25 mins
9	4	5	-	5	4	4-4½ hrs	-	1	20-25 mins
10	5	6	4½	6	5	4¼-4¾ hrs	1	-	25-30 mins
11	6	7	-	7	6	4½-5 hrs	-	1½	25-30 mins
12	7	8	6½	8	7	5-5½ hrs	1½	-	25-30 mins

Template graph and instructions.

(Do not remove or draw directly onto this graph.)

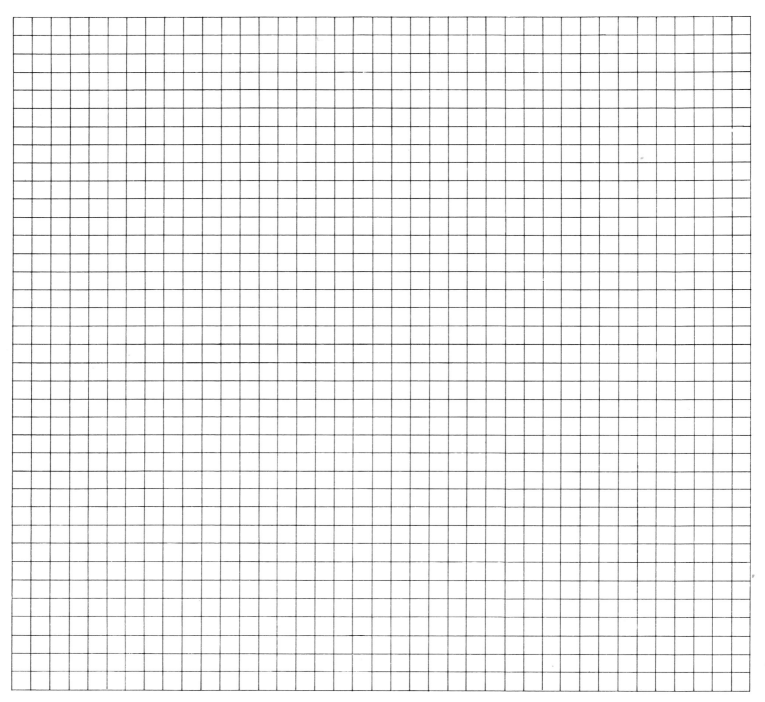

Explanatory note:
Most cakes in this book include artwork necessitating the use of graphs (for an example please refer to the drawing of the lily template in picture No.1 of the cake 'Renita' on page 16). All graphs, such as that in picture No.1, need to be adjusted to obtain the correct scale. this can be achieved by using the following instructions.

Instructions:
1. Count and record the number of squares in picture No.1.
2. Cover the TEMPLATE GRAPH with a sheet of greaseproof paper and count out, mark and trace the equivalent number of squares on the greaseproof paper.
3. Remove the greaseproof paper graph and return to page 16.

4. Wherever the drawing in picture No.1 crosses a line, mark the identical crossing point on the greaseproof paper graph.
5. Still using the picture as a guide, join the marks on the greaseproof paper graph to re-create drawing No.1 on page 16.

Equipment.

Turntable	Straight edge	Plain scraper	Flower nail
6" Palette knife	Rolling pin	Serrated scraper	Edible colourings
4" Palette knife	Pair of marzipan spacers	Nylon piping bag	Icing tubes

The above are the items of equipment used in making the cakes that appear in our book. Most of them were designed by us, and they are all obtainable through the Company's Mail Order Department.

You will find each item, and many more, featured in our catalogue, which can be obtained from:

Mary Ford Cake Artistry Centre Ltd.
28–30 Southbourne Grove, Southbourne,
Bournemouth BH6 3RA.

**Cake decorating courses are held at the Mary Ford Centre.
For further details please apply to the above address**

Mary Ford Tube No.'s showing their shapes.

0 1 2 3 4 5 6 7 13 22 32 42 43 44 57 58 59

The above are all the icing tubes used in this book.
Please note that these are Mary Ford tubes, but comparable tubes may be used.

Piped Designs.

1. 1st stage of 6-dot sequence, pipe 3 dots.
2. 2nd stage, pipe 2 further dots.
3. 3rd stage, pipe last dot to complete sequence.
4. Graduated bulbs.
5. Shell.
6. Cone-shaped shell.
7. Rosette.
8. 'C' line.
9. Bold 'C'.
10. 'S' line.
11. Rope.
12. Curved rope.
13. Spiral shell.
14. 'C' scroll.
15. 'S' scroll.
16. Left-to-right scroll.
17. Right-to-left scroll.

Various Writing Styles.

ABCDEFGHIJKLMNOPQRSTUVWXYZ ÆØ 1234567890

ABCDEFGHIJKLMNOPQRSTUVWXYZ ÆØ 1234567890

A ABCDEE FGHIJ KLM NOPQRR STTUVWXYZ

ABCDEEFGHIJKLLMNOPQRSTUVWXYZ 12345678890

ABCDEFGHIJKLMNOPQRSTUVWXYZ 1234567890

ABCDEFGHIJKLMNOPQRSTUVWXYZ 1234567890

ABCDEFGHIJKLMNOPQRSTUVWXYZ ÆØ 1234567890

ABCDEFGHIJKLMNOPQRSTUVWXYZ

ABCDEFGHIJKLMNOPQRSTUVWXYZ 1234567890

ABCDEFGHIJKLMNOPQRSTUVWXYZ 1234567890

ABCDEFGHIJKLMNOPQRSTUVWXYZ 1234567890

ABCDEFGHIJKLMNOPQRSTUVWXYZ

Making and filling a greaseproof piping bag

1. A sheet of greaseproof paper – 12″×8″ – required.

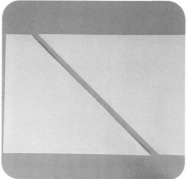
2. Cut sheet diagonally as shown.

3. Turn one triangle to position shown.

4. Fold paper from right to centre.

5. Lift corner from left to right.

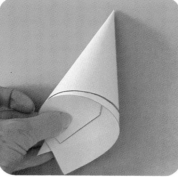
6. Fold under and pull into shape.

7. Fold in loose ends and cut section. Fold back to secure.

8. Cut off tip of bag and drop in tube.

9. Using a palette knife, half fill bag with Royal Icing.

10. Carefully fold and roll the open end to seal bag, which is then ready for use.

11. To make a LEAF BAG repeat 1–7 and then flatten tip.

12. Picture showing shape of tip to be cut.

13. Now cut tip.

14. For using TWO COLOURS partially fill one side of bag with one colour.

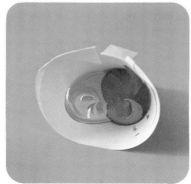
15. Fill remaining half with 2nd colour. Repeat 10.

16. Picture showing effect of using two colours of Royal Icing.

How to marzipan

17. Picture showing a matured fruit cake with lining paper removed.

18. Upturn cake, place on board (3″ larger) and if required brush on spirits and glycerine.

19. Using icing sugar for dusting, roll marzipan between spacers (approx: ⅜″ thick), as shown.

20. Cut marzipan to size using the cake tin (in which the cake was baked) as guide.

21. After removing surplus marzipan brush off any loose icing sugar.

22. Jam the marzipan with boiling apricot puree by applying it with a palette knife.

23. Lay cake onto the jammed marzipan.

24. Upturn cake and replace on board.

25. Picture showing a square cake (which is prepared in the same way as a round cake).

26. Form remaining marzipan into a sausage shape.

27. Now roll the marzipan into a thin strip (wide enough to cover the cake side).

28. Cut marzipan for side (length=approx: 3 times diameter) and then jam as in 22.

29. Fix marzipan to cake side and trim off surplus (L.D. approx: 3 days).

30. For a square cake roll out a sheet of marzipan to cover the 4 sides.

31. Cut the sheet into 4 separate strips to fit sides.

32. Jam and fix each strip then trim (L.D. approx: 3 days).

HOW TO CUT A WEDGE
33. After marzipanning, cut wedge from cake, as shown.

34. Replace wedge.

35. Mark board to show position of wedge. Place cake on turntable.

HOW TO COAT A CAKE
36. Spread Royal Icing around side of cake with a palette knife.

37. Place hands in position shown (holding the scraper against the cake side).

38. Holding scraper steady with one hand, revolve the turntable one complete turn with the other hand.

39. Repeat 36–38 until side is smooth.

40. Using the palette knife, remove surplus icing fom cake.

41. Immediately remove wedge.

42. Clean sides of wedge and replace (L.D. 12 hrs).

43. Using the palette knife, place Royal Icing on top of the cake.

44. Using the palette knife in a paddling movement, spread the icing evenly over the cake top.

45. Using a stainless steel rule, start to level the icing.

46. Continue to use the rule in a backwards and forwards motion to level icing.

47. Picture showing coated cake.

48. Remove surplus icing from edges of cake top and wedge (L.D. 12 hrs). Repeat 36–48 twice more.

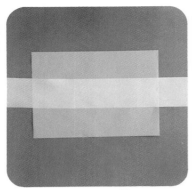

49. 1½ yards of satin ribbon on a piece of greaseproof paper – approx: 8″×6″ required.

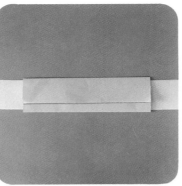

50. Fold the paper over the centre of the ribbon.

51. Fold the paper and ribbon in half and place to wedge.

52. Replace wedge.

53. Roll up equal lengths of ribbon ends and fix to side of cake.

HOW TO COAT A BOARD.
54. Picture showing hands and scraper in readiness to coat board.

55. Holding scraper steady in one hand, revolve the turntable one complete turn with the other (see picture 38).

56. For coating a square (or hexagonal, etc.) cake, coat the opposite sides (L.D. 12 hrs).

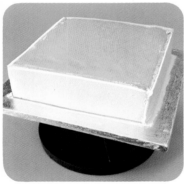

57. Now coat remaining sides (L.D. 12 hrs).

58. Coat the top as for round cake (L.D. 12 hrs). Repeat 56–58 twice more.

HOW TO MAKE A SUGAR PASTE ROSE BUD.
59. Roll a piece of sugar paste into the shape shown.

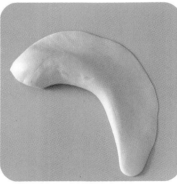

60. Flatten back to form sharp edge.

61. Roll up the sugar paste as shown.

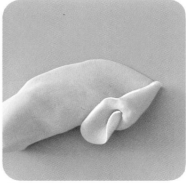

62. Continue rolling, as shown.

63. Fold over remaining sugar paste.

64. Remove surplus sugar paste, then bend back edge to form bud.

HOW TO MAKE A SUGAR PASTE ROSE.
65. Repeat 59–64 but finishing with bud in upright position.

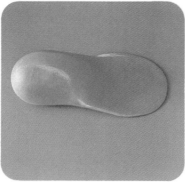

66. Roll out sugar paste and flatten one end.

67. Cut away surplus leaving the petal.

68. Wrap petal around the bud and slightly dampen with water to fix.

69. Repeat 66–68 for the second petal.

70. Repeat 66–68 making and fixing larger petals until size of rose required is obtained.

MAKING ROYAL ICING BIRDS.
71. Pipe wings on waxed paper, working from left to right (No.1) (L.D. 12 hrs).

72. Pipe tail on waxed paper (two types shown) (No.1).

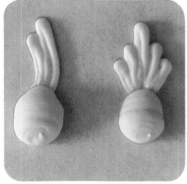

73. Pipe body against tail (No.1).

74. Lifting icing bag pipe neck, head and beak (No.1).

75. Immediately fix wings to body (L.D. 12 hrs).

MAKING SUGAR BELLS
76. Pipe a bulb on waxed paper (No.3).

77. Pipe a second bulb on top (No.3).

78. Sprinkle granulated sugar over the bulbs (then leave until outside of bulbs are dry).

79. Scoop out unset Royal Icing from centre of bell.

80. Pipe-in hammer (No.1).

PIPING SUGAR FLOWERS & ROSES

PIPING SUGAR FLOWERS
81. Picture showing items required=flower nail, waxed paper and piping bag with petal tube (No.58).

82. Fix a square of waxed paper to top of flower nail and hold in position shown.

83. Keeping thick end of tube to the centre of flower, pipe 1st petal.

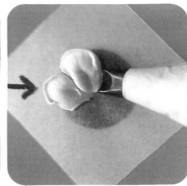

84. Turn nail and pipe next petal.

85. Turn nail and pipe 3rd petal.

86. Turn nail and pipe 4th petal.

87. Turn nail and pipe 5th petal.

88. Turn nail and pipe the last petal.

89. Picture showing the piped petals.

90. Pipe a centre bulb (No.2) (L.D. 24 hrs).

PIPING SUGAR ROSES
91. Form a cone of marzipan.

92. Using stiff Royal Icing, pipe the centre of the rose (No.57).

93. Pipe a petal behind the centre (No.57).

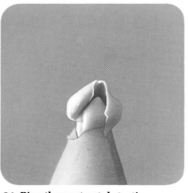

94. Pipe the next petal starting inside the 1st petal (No.57).

95. Pipe the 3rd petal, starting inside the 2nd petal and ending over part of the 1st petal (No.57) (L.D. 15 m).

96. Repeat 93–95 for 5 petals around outside of rose (L.D. 24 hrs). Remove from cone.

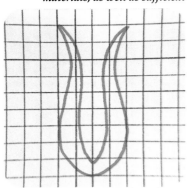

1. Drawing showing template of lily petals.

2. Outline lily petals on waxed paper.

3. Flood-in lily petals.

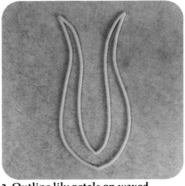

4. Immediately place on curved piece of tin. (5 required) (L.D. 2 hrs).

5. Outline and flood-in on waxed paper a 1" diameter disc (L.D. 24 hrs).

6. Outline and flood-in the centre-piece lily petal, as shown (L.D. 30m).

7. Pipe a bulb at the base of each centre-piece (No.2) (L.D. 24 hrs).

8. Pipe four pairs of bird wings on waxed paper (No.1) (L.D. 30m).

9. Pipe a curved line on each wing, as shown (No.1).

10. Pipe shells around cake-top edge in position shown (No.2).

11. Support cake upside down in position shown.

12. Pipe loops inside cake-top shells (No.1).

13. Pipe a larger loop on cake-edge, as shown (No.2).

14. Continue piping loops around cake-edge (No.2).

15. Pipe a spike between each outer loop (No.2) (L.D. 20m).

16. Upturn cake.

16

17. Pipe shells around cake-base (No.2).

18. Support cake upside down as in picture 11. Pipe loops around cake-board, as shown (No.2).

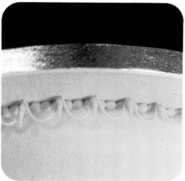

19. Pipe a spike between each loop (No.2) (L.D. 20m).

20. Upturn cake.

21. Pipe a bulb at the base of each spike (No.1).

22. Pipe two rows of shells around cake-board, as shown (No.2).

23. Pipe a line on the cake-board shells shown (No.1).

24. Pipe bird's heads and back wings on cake side, as shown (No.1) (T).

25. Pipe a body and tail to each bird (No.1) (T).

26. Fix a runout wing to each bird. (Repeat 24–26 around cake-side, as required).

27. Pipe floral stem on cake-board, as shown (No.1).

28. Pipe cone shaped whirls on stem, as shown (No.1). (Repeat 27 and 28 around cake-board, as required).

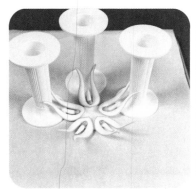

29. Fix and support lily petals to runout disc (L.D. 4 hrs).

30. Fix artificial decorations of choice to centre of lily.

31. Form and fix a sugar paste base to cake-top and cover side with matching ribbon.

32. Fix lily to sugar paste base.

Adeline

1. Cut a square of paper exactly ⅓rd the length and width of the cake and place on top.

2. Pipe a line around the paper square (No.1) remove the paper.

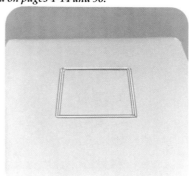

3. Pipe a line outside the No.1 line (No.2).

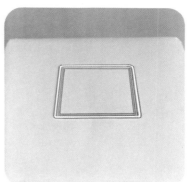

4. Pipe a line outside the No.2 line (No.3).

5. Overpipe the No.2 line (No.1).

6. Overpipe the No.3 line (No.2).

7. Overpipe the No.2 line (No.1).

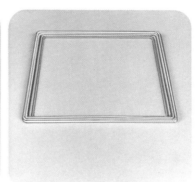

8. Pipe a 'V', as shown, from each corner of the central square (No.2).

9. Pipe a curved line to connect each 'V' (No.2).

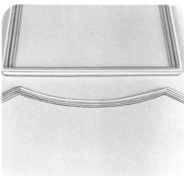

10. Pipe a line beside the No.2 line and then overpipe the No.2 line (No.1).

11. Pipe an elongated heart shape at each cake top corner (No.4).

12. Overpipe each heart shape (No.3).

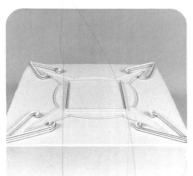

13. Overpipe each heart shape (No.2) and then overpipe each heart shape (No.1).

14. Pipe 'S' scrolls, as shown, around top edges of cake (No.4).

15. Beneath each scroll pipe a shorter 'S' scroll (No.4).

16. Pipe 'S' scrolls, as shown, around cake base (No.4) (T).

19

17. Pipe 'S' scrolls, as shown, on cake board (No.4) (T).

18. Pipe 'C' scrolls at each cake-side corner (No.4) (T).

19. Pipe a spiral shell between base scrolls (No.4).

20. Overpipe each top scroll (No.3).

21. Overpipe each base scroll (No.3).

22. Overpipe each spiral shell with 2 curved lines (No.3).

23. Pipe 5 curved lines around each side of cake, as shown (No.3) (T).

24. Overpipe each top scroll (No.2).

25. Overpipe each base scroll and spiral shell (No.2).

26. Pipe a line under each No.3 curved line on cake sides (No.2) and then against each No.3 line (No.2) (T).

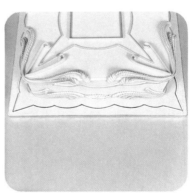

27. Pipe, as shown, a series of curved lines and 'V's on cake board (No.2).

28. Overpipe each top scroll, base scroll and spiral shell (No.1).

29. Pipe a line under each No.2 line on the cake side and then against each No.2 line (No.1) (T).

30. Pipe a line beside each No.2 line on the board and then overpipe each No.2 line (No.1).

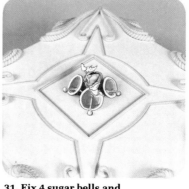

31. Fix 4 sugar bells and decorations of choice at centre top of cake.

32. Fix decorations of choice to cake, as shown.

NOTE: *Before attempting to decorate this cake, please study the whole sequence of photographs and notes and ensure you have the proper equipment and materials, as well as sufficient time. Additional information can be found on pages 4-14 and 96.*

1. Mark each top-edge of cake into six equal portions with piped dots.

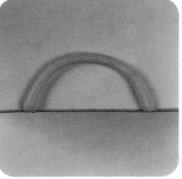

2. Join two dots with piped half-circle (No.3).

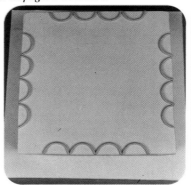

3. Continue piping half-circles, as shown.

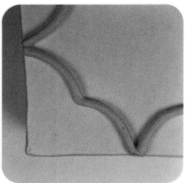

4. Pipe two curved lines at each cake-top corner (No.3).

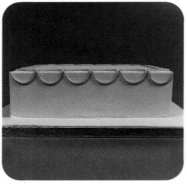

5. Pipe half-circles around cake-side, as shown (No.3) (T).

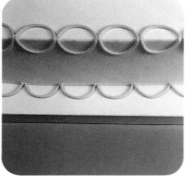

6. Pipe half-circles on cake-board, as shown (No.3).

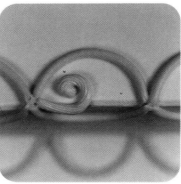

7. Pipe 'C' scroll on cake-top edge, as shown (No.43).

8. Pipe adjoining 'C' scroll, as shown (No.43). Repeat 7 and 8 in half-circles on cake-top.

9. Pipe large bulb in centre of half-circle at cake-base (No.3).

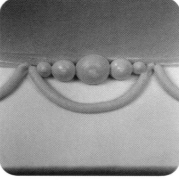

10. Pipe graduated bulbs, as shown (No.3). Repeat 9 and 10 around cake-base (No.3).

11. Overpipe 'C' scroll (No.3).

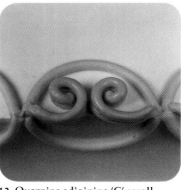

12. Overpipe adjoining 'C' scroll (No.3). Continue 11 and 12 around cake-top.

13. Pipe a line beside the No.3 line on cake-top, as shown (No.2).

14. Overpipe the No.3 line on cake-top (No.2).

15. Overpipe the 'C' scrolls (No.2).

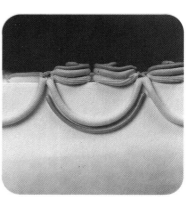

16. Pipe a line under each No.3 line on cake-sides (No.2) (T).

17. Pipe a line against the No.3 line on cake sides (No.2) (T).

18. Pipe a line beside each No.3 line on cake-board (No.2).

19. Overpipe the No.3 line on cake-board (No.2).

20. Pipe a line beside each No.2 line on cake-top (No.1).

21. Overpipe each No.2 line, as shown (No.1).

22. Overpipe each No.2 line, as shown (No.1).

23. Overpipe each 'C' scroll (No.1).

24. Repeat 20, 21 and 22 on each cake-side (T).

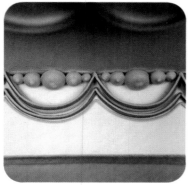

25. Repeat 20, 21 and 22 on cake-board.

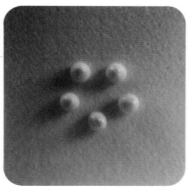

26. Pipe flower motif in each half-circle on cake-side (No.1) (T).

27. Complete each flower motif, as shown (No.1) (T).

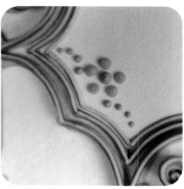

28. Pipe flower motif at each cake-top corner as shown (No.1).

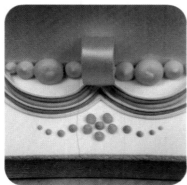

29. Pipe flower motif to each board centre (No.1) and fix roll of ribbon in position shown.

30. Pipe flower motif on decoration of choice (No.1) – i.e. slipper.

31. Fix curled ribbon to centre of cake bottom tier. Decorate as shown (No.1).

32. Fix decorations of choice to cake corners.

23

Primrose

1. Drawing showing template of large heart.

2. Drawing showing template of medium heart.

3. Drawing showing template of small heart.

4. Outline and flood-in on waxed paper one of each sized heart (L.D. 24 hrs).

5. Make 9 love-birds.

6. Pipe primrose petal on waxed paper (No.57).

7. Pipe second petal (No.57).

8. Pipe third petal (No.57).

9. Pipe fourth petal (No.57).

10. Pipe fifth petal to complete primrose (No.57) (L.D. 12 hrs) (66 required).

11. Lightly brush edible colouring from centre of each flower.

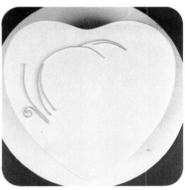

12. Pipe curved lines on cake-top, as shown (No.1) and then over-pipe the No.1 lines (No.1).

13. Pipe further curved lines (No.1) and then overpipe the further curved lines (No.1).

14. Pipe inscription of choice (No.1) and then overpipe inscription (No.1).

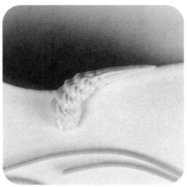

15. Pipe a 'C' scroll from right to left at centre of cake-top edge (No.42).

16. Pipe 3 graduated bulbs in position shown (No.2).

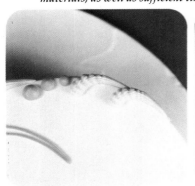

17. Pipe 2 'C' scrolls in position shown (No.42).

18. Pipe 2 graduated bulbs in position shown (No.2).

19. Pipe alternate 'C' scrolls (No.42) and bulbs (No.2), as shown.

20. Repeat 15–19 from left to right, as shown.

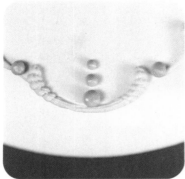

21. Pipe 2 'C' scrolls (No.42) and 3 graduated bulbs (No.2) at cake-top front edge.

22. Pipe bulbs around cake-base except where shown (No.3).

23. Overpipe each cake-top scroll (No.2).

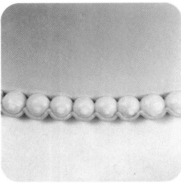

24. Pipe a line against each cake-base bulb (No.2).

25. Fix hearts to cake-top and a primrose to each heart.

26. Fix lovebirds and decorations of choice to cake-top.

27. Fix loops of primroses around cake-side.

28. Pipe lines and a heart to cake-board front (No.2) and fix decorations.

29. Pipe a heart on cake-board (No.2) and then pipe a line outside the No.2 line (No.1).

30. Pipe lines, as shown (No.1) and then fix decorations. Repeat 29 and 30 around cake-board, as required.

31 Pipe 2 curved lines between each pair of hearts (No.2).

32. Overpipe each No.2 curved line (No.1) and fix decoration of choice, as shown.

26

NOTE: Before attempting to decorate this cake, please study the whole sequence of photographs and notes and ensure you have the proper equipment and materials, as well as sufficient time. Additional information can be found on pages 4-14 and 96.

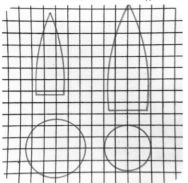

1. Drawing of templates for lily petals and centre. (6 of each petal and 1 of each disc required).

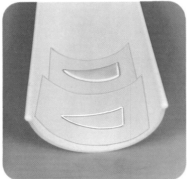

2. Outline and flood-in all petals and discs and place petals in curved mould (L.D. 24 hrs).

3. Mark top of cake into 18 equal spaces with small piped dots (No.1).

4. Immediately beneath top dots, mark base of cake with piped dots (No.1).

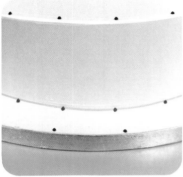

5. Repeat on outer edge of board (No.1).

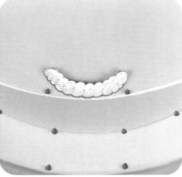

6. Pipe curved rope mark to mark around top of cake (No.44).

7. Repeat on board (No.44). (Ensure marker dots are hidden).

8. Starting with centre bulb, graduate either side (No.3).

9. Overpipe further rope on 1st rope on top of cake (No.3).

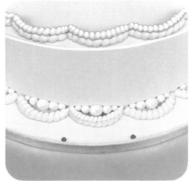

10. Overpipe further rope on base rope (No.3).

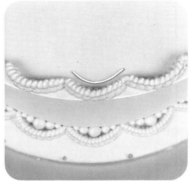

11. Pipe a line inside curve of rope on top of cake (No.2).

12. Overpipe further rope on 2nd rope (No.2).

13. Pipe curved line directly below each rope (No.2) (T).

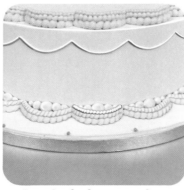

14. Overpipe further rope on base 2nd rope (No.2).

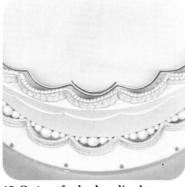

15. On top of cake drop line by side of No.2 (No.1).

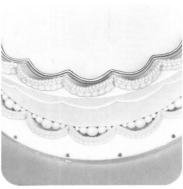

16. Overpipe on top of No.2 (No.1).

28

NOTE: Before attempting to decorate this cake, please study the whole sequence of photographs and notes and ensure you have the proper equipment and materials, as well as sufficient time. Additional information can be found on pages 4-14 and 96.

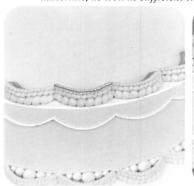

17. Overpipe further rope on 3rd rope (No.1).

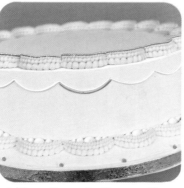

18. Pipe a line under No.2 on side of cake (No.1) (T).

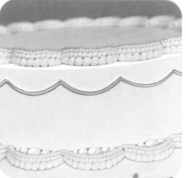

19. Continuing on side of cake, pipe against No.2 (No.1) (T).

20. Overpipe further rope on 3rd base rope (No.1).

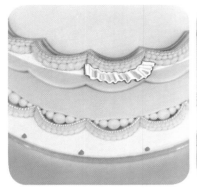

21. Using stiff icing, pipe frill against No.44 using wide end of tube nearest cake. Pipe right to left (No.58).

22. Repeat against base rope (No.58).

23. Pipe a line onto board, following curve of frill (No.2).

24. Pipe a line beside the No.2 line (No.1). Carefully scrape off marker dots on edge of board.

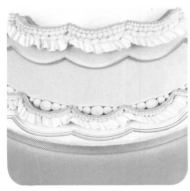

25. Pipe a line on top of the No.2 line (No.1).

26. Pipe three graduated dots at joins (No.1).

27. Make and secure a sugar paste base to support lily. Pipe plain shells around edge (No.2).

28. Fix larger disc to sugar paste base. Fix 6 large petals around edge. Finish with shells (No.2).

29. Fix smaller petals on top and in between larger petals.

30. Fix smaller disc in centre, hiding base of petals, and pipe small icing spikes between petals (No.1).

31. Pipe small spikes to edge of disc (No.1). Using artificial flowers of choice, fix to centre of lily.

32. Complete cake with matching flowers, silver leaves and silver ribbon.

Georgina

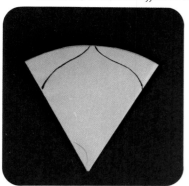

1. Fold a 4½″ diameter circle of paper into 6 and then draw the lines shown on top section.

2. Cut paper along curved lines, unfold and place on cake-top.

3. Pipe scrolls beside the paper template, as shown (No. 42) and then remove template.

4. Pipe curved lines at each pair of scroll tails, as shown (No. 42).

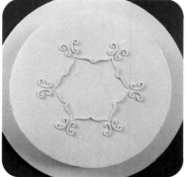

5. Picture showing cake-top.

6. Pipe 'S' lines, as shown (No. 42).

7. Pipe straight lines around cake-top design, as shown (No. 3).

8. Pipe floral motif at each pair of 'S' lines (No. 2).

9. Overpipe each scroll (No. 2).

10. Overpipe each curved and 'S' line (No. 2).

11. Pipe a line beside each cake-top No. 3 line (No. 2) and then overpipe each No. 3 line (No. 2).

12. Overpipe each scroll, 'S' line and curved line (No. 1).

13. Pipe a line beside each No. 2 line (No. 1) and then overpipe each No. 2 line (No. 1).

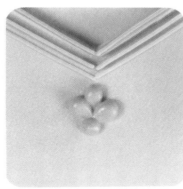

14. Pipe floral motif at each corner (No. 2).

15. Pipe lines around cake-top design, as shown (No. 2).

16. Pipe a line beside the outside No. 2 line (No. 1) and then overpipe the No. 2 line (No. 1).

NOTE: *Before attempting to decorate this cake, please study the whole sequence of photographs and notes and ensure you have the proper equipment and materials, as well as sufficient time. Additional information can be found on pages 4-14 and 96.*

17. Pipe a pair of scrolls at each corner, as shown (No.43).

18. Pipe curved lines between each pair of outer scrolls (No.43).

19. Pipe pairs of scrolls in position shown around cake-top edge. (No.43) (T).

20. Pipe a floral motif at cake-base below the centre of each pair of cake-edge scrolls (No.2) (T).

21. Pipe a line around cake-base between each floral motif (No.43) (L.D. 15m).

22. Pipe a pair of scrolls over each cake-base No.43 line (No.43).

23. Pipe curved lines around cake-side centre, as shown (No.3) (T).

24. Overpipe each No. 43 scroll and curved line (No.3) (T· as necessary).

25. Pipe a line beneath each cake-side No.3 line (No.2) and then overpipe each No.3 line (No.2) (T).

26. Overpipe each No.3 scroll and curved line (No.2) (T as necessary).

27. Pipe a line beneath each cake-side No.2 line (No.1) and then overpipe each No.2 line (No.1) (T).

28. Overpipe each No.2 scroll and curved line (No.1) (T as necessary).

29. Pipe curved lines in position shown on cake-board (No.42) and repeat around board.

30. Pipe lines shown around cake-board (No.3).

31. Pipe a line beside each cake-board No.3 line (No.2) and over-pipe each cake-board No.43 and No.3 line (No.2).

32. Pipe a line beside each cake-board No.2 line (No.1) and over-pipe each cake-board No.2 line (No.1).

1. Drawing showing template of double-bell.

2. Outline double-bell on waxed paper (No.1) (4 required for each tier).

3. Flood-in areas shown (L.D. 30 m).

4. Flood-in further areas shown (L.D. 30 m).

5. Flood-in further areas shown (L.D. 30 m).

6. Complete flooding-in (L.D. 24 hrs).

7. Pipe 4 curved lines along each side of the cake top, as shown (No.1).

8. Pipe reverse curved lines on board (No.1).

9. Pipe an angled line between the No.1 line and the cake edge (No.1).

10. Continue piping lines at same angle within the patterned area around cake top.

11. Picture showing cake top pattern complete with angled lines.

12. Pipe a line in the opposite direction, as shown (No.1).

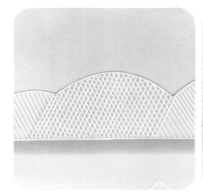

13. Continue piping lines at same angle within the patterned area around cake top.

14. Picture showing cake top pattern complete with angled lines.

15. Repeat 9–13 on board pattern, as shown.

16. Pipe plain shells on cake top curved lines (No.2).

34

NOTE: Before attempting to decorate this cake, please study the whole sequence of photographs and notes and ensure you have the proper equipment and materials, as well as sufficient time. Additional information can be found on pages 4–14 and 96.

17. Pipe a line beside the shells (No.2).

18. Pipe a line beside the No.2 line and then overpipe the No.2 line (No.1).

19. Pipe plain shells on board curved lines (No.2).

20. Pipe shells around base of cake (No.42).

21. Pipe an 'S' scroll on cake top edge (No.42).

22. Pipe a 'C' scroll over line-work on cake top (No.42).

23. Pipe another 'S' scroll on top edge of cake (No.42).

24. Repeat 21–23 from opposite corner of same cake top edge. Then repeat along each edge.

25. Overpipe the scrolls (No.2).

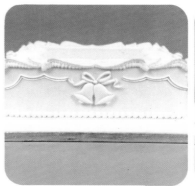

26. Pipe a line beside the board No.2 shells (No.2).

27. Pipe a line beside the board No.2 line and then overpipe the No.2 line (No.1).

28. Overpipe the scrolls (No.1).

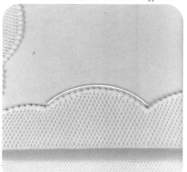

29. Fix bell runouts to each side of cake.

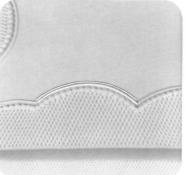

30. Pipe curved lines on side of cake, as shown (No.2) (T).

31. Pipe a line under the cake-side No.2 line then against the No.2 line (No.1) (T).

32. Fix sugar doves, artificial flowers of choice and ribbon, as shown.

Daisy

36

1. Pipe 1st petal of a daisy on waxed paper (No.57).

2. Continue piping tight petals in clockwise direction.

3. Continue piping tight petals.

4. Complete circle of petals.

5. Complete daisy with yellow centre (No.2) (135 daisies required) (L.D. 24 hrs).

6. Make 12 sugar bells (No.3) (see instructions).

7. Pipe 4 dots at points on diagonal line (corner to corner).

8. Divide top of cake into 3 and pipe 2 dots between existing dots but closer to cake centre.

9. Pipe 2 further dots on cake board. (They must be in line with the 2 middle dots on cake top). Repeat around cake.

10. Pipe curved lines from outer dots to inner dots (No.3).

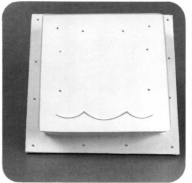

11. Join the outer lines with central curved line (No.3).

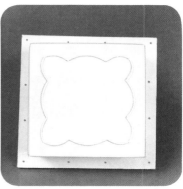

12. Repeat No's.10–11 around the top of the cake (No.3).

13. Pipe equal curves on each side around the cake board (No.3).

14. Pipe a line inside the No.3 line around the cake top (No.2).

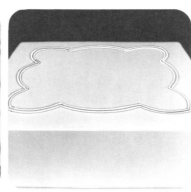

15. Overpipe the No.3 line around the top of cake (No.2).

16. Pipe a line outside the No.3 line around the board and then pipe a line on top of the No.3 line (No.2).

NOTE: Before attempting to decorate this cake, please study the whole sequence of photographs and notes and ensure you have the proper equipment and materials, as well as sufficient time. Additional information can be found on pages 4-14 and 96.

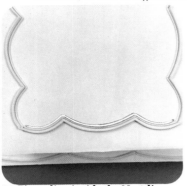

17. Pipe a line inside the No.2 line on top of the cake (No.1).

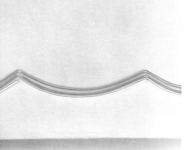

18. Pipe a line on top of the middle line on top of the cake (No.1).

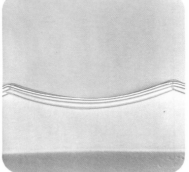

19. Pipe a line on top of outer line on cake top (No.1).

20. Pipe a line on cake board outside the No.2 line and then overpipe both No.2 lines (No.1).

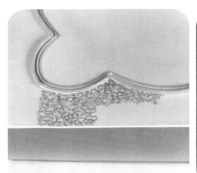

21. Filigree outer edge of top of cake (No.1).

22. Filigree inside pattern on cake board (No.1).

23. Pipe plain shells around top edge of cake (No.4).

24. Pipe plain shells around base of cake (No.4).

25. Pipe 4 graduated dots at each pattern corner, both on cake top and board (No.1).

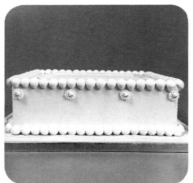

26. Fix 4 equally spaced daisies on each side of cake.

27. Join each central daisy pair with a curve of daisies.

28. Join further daisy curves to form chain around the cake.

29. Fix 3 daisies to centre top of cake.

30. Fix bells on top of cake at pattern corners.

31. Fix single daisies at cake base.

32. Fix artificial wishbone at each base corner.

Patricia

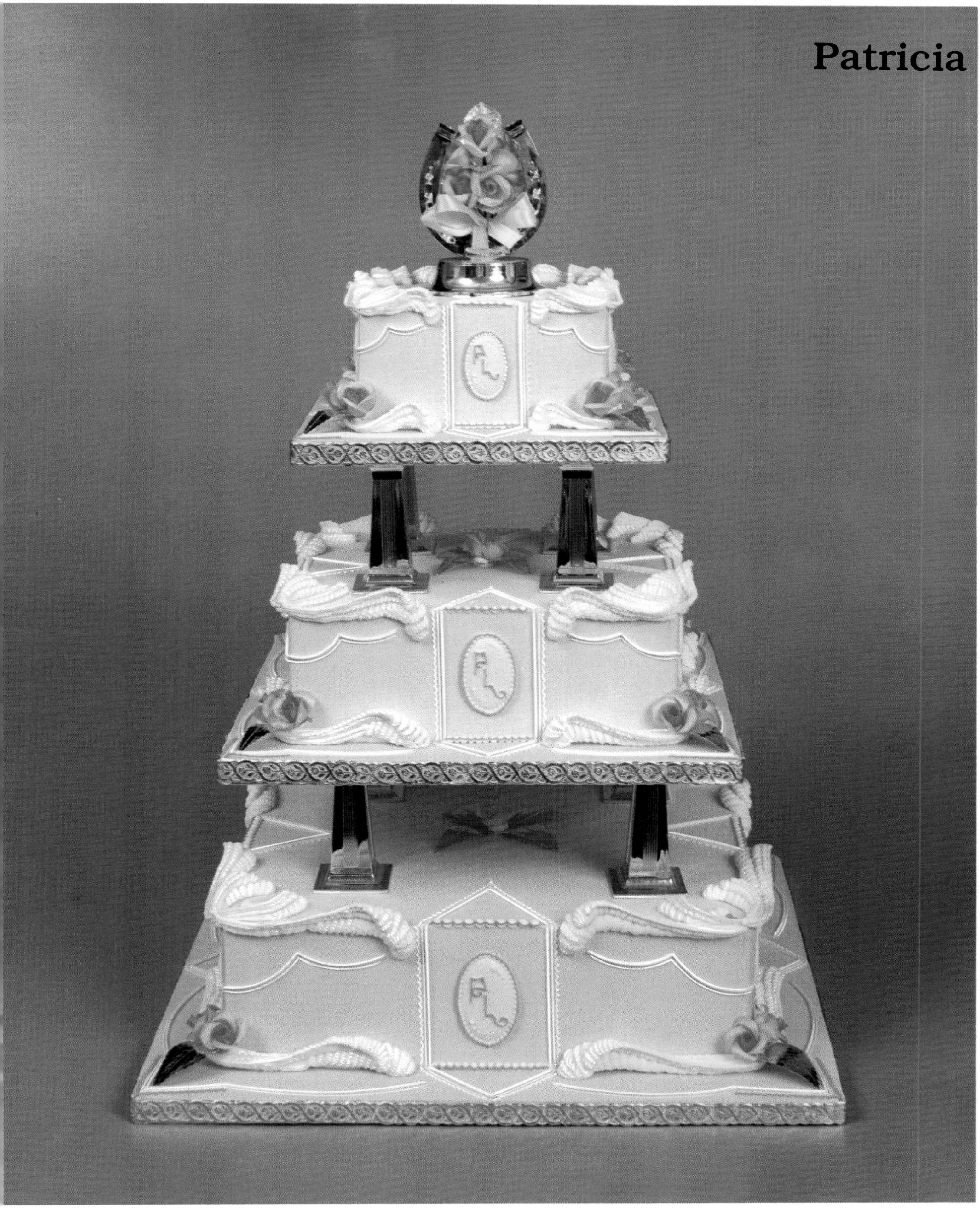

NOTE: Before attempting to decorate this cake, please study the whole sequence of photographs and notes and ensure you have the proper equipment and materials, as well as sufficient time. Additional information can be found on pages 4-14 and 96.

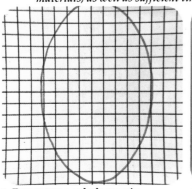

1. Runout 12 oval plaques in proportion to cake sizes (see full cake photograph). (L.D. 24 hrs).

2. Pipe 4 marker dots on cake top (No.1).

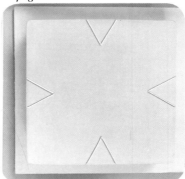

3. Pipe lines to form 'V's on each cake top edge (No.2).

4. Follow 'V' lines down cake sides (No.2). (T).

5. Pipe 'V's on board to form pattern (No.2).

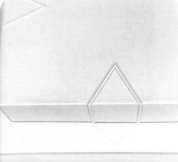

6. Pipe a line beside the No.2 lines on cake top (No.1).

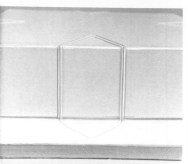

7. Continue lines down cake sides (No.1) (T).

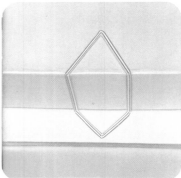

8. Continue lines on board (No.1).

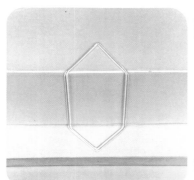

9. Overpipe a line on all No.2 lines (No.1) (T as necessary).

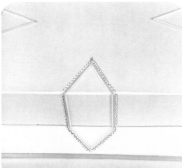

10. Pipe a scallop beside all the No.1 lines and finish 'V's with 3 graduated dots (No.1) (T as necessary).

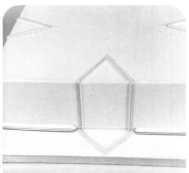

11. Pipe a line around cake base, excluding 'V's (No.44).

12. Pipe a scroll from 'V' to right-hand corner (No.44).

13. Pipe a 'C' scroll to right-hand cake corner (No.44).

14. Pipe a scroll from 'V' to left-hand corner (No.44).

15. Pipe a 'C' scroll to left-hand cake corner (No.44).

16. Pipe left and right-handed scrolls to base corner (No.44). (Repeat 12–16 at each corner).

NOTE: *Before attempting to decorate this cake, please study the whole sequence of photographs and notes and ensure you have the proper equipment and materials, as well as sufficient time. Additional information can be found on pages 4-14 and 96.*

17. Overpipe each cake-top scroll (No.3).

18. Overpipe each base scroll (No.3).

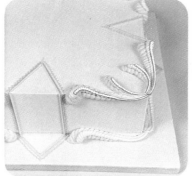

19. Overpipe each No.3 cake-top scroll (No.2).

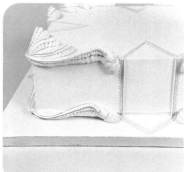

20. Overpipe each No.3 base scroll (No.2).

21. Overpipe each No.2 cake-top scroll (No.1).

22. Overpipe each No.2 base scroll (No.1).

23. Pipe curved lines under each scroll on cake side (No.2) (T).

24. Pipe a line under and then pipe a line against each No.2 line on cake side (No.1) (T).

25. Pipe a 'V' and then a curved line on each corner of board (No.2).

26. Pipe a line on the board beside each No.2 line and then overpipe each No.2 line (No.1).

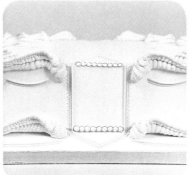

27. Pipe small plain shells on cake-top edge and base (No.2).

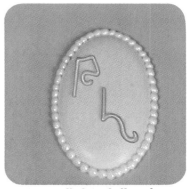

28. Pipe small plain shells and initials on each plaque (No.1) (L.D. 12 hrs).

29. Overpipe the shells and initials in coloured Royal Icing (No.1) (L.D. 2 hrs).

30. Fix plaque to each side of cake and finish with decorative dots.

31. Pipe corner motif with coloured Royal Icing (No.1) and then overpipe shells (No.1).

32. Pipe a scallop at each corner 'V' (No.1) and then fix decoration of choice.

Greta

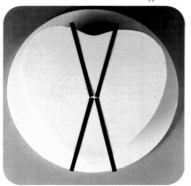

1. Cut four strips of card and place on cake-top, as shown.

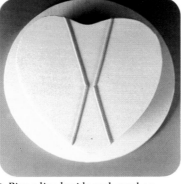

2. Pipe a line beside each marker card (No.4) and then remove cards.

3. Pipe vertical and base lines at front and back of cake, as shown (No.4) (T).

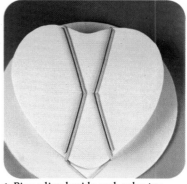

4. Pipe a line beside each cake-top line (No.4).

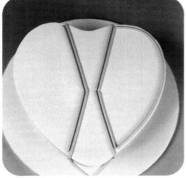

5. Pipe a line 1/4" inside cake-top rim (No.4), as shown.

6. Pipe a line 1/4" inside cake-top rim (No.4), as shown.

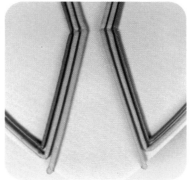

7. Pipe a line inside each cake-top pattern (No.3).

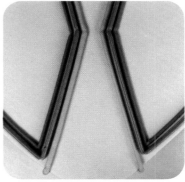

8. Overpipe the No.4 line shown (No.3).

9. Equally divide each cake-side panel and mark with piped dots.

10. Pipe a curved line between each pair of marker dots (No.3) (T).

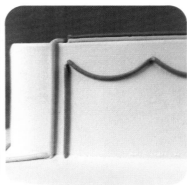

11. Pipe a line beside each vertical cake-side line (No.3) (T).

12. Pipe a line inside each cake-top pattern (No.2).

13. Overpipe the inner cake-top No.3 line (No.2).

14. Overpipe the outer cake-top No.3 line (No.2).

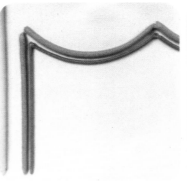

15. Pipe a line beside each cake-side No.3 line (No.2) (T).

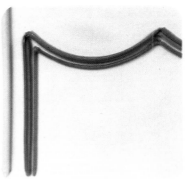

16. Pipe a line against each cake-side No.3 line (No.2) (T).

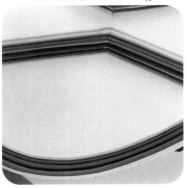

17. Pipe a line inside each cake-top pattern (No.1).

18. Overpipe each cake-top No.2 line (No.1).

19. Pipe a line under each cake-side No.2 line (No.1) (T).

20. Pipe a line against each cake-side No.2 line (No.1) (T).

21. Pipe matching curved lines on cake-board (No.1).

22. Pipe a line beside each cake-board curved line (No.2).

23. Overpipe each cake-board No.2 line (No.1).

24. Pipe a line beside each cake-board No.2 line (No.3).

25. Overpipe each cake-board No.3 line (No.2).

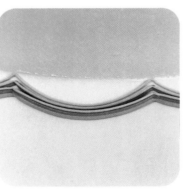

26. Overpipe each cake-board No.2 line (No.1).

27. Pipe graduated bulbs in each cake-board curved line (No.3).

28. Filigree central panel (No.1) (T as necessary).

29. Pipe a line around cake-board, as shown (No.4).

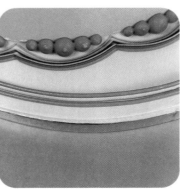

30. Pipe a line beside the No.4 line (No.3) and overpipe the No.4 line (No.3).

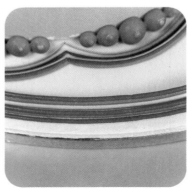

31. Pipe a line beside the No.3 line (No.2) and overpipe each No.3 line (No.2).

32. Pipe a line beside the No.2 line (No.1) and overpipe the No.2 line (No.1).

NOTE: Before attempting to decorate this cake, please study the whole sequence of photographs and notes and ensure you have the proper equipment and materials, as well as sufficient time. Additional information can be found on pages 4-14 and 96.

1. Drawing showing template of corner decoration.

2. Pipe curved line on waxed paper, as shown (No.4) (L.D. 2 hrs) (6 required for each tier).

3. Pipe 2nd line so that the bottom of the 1st line is overpiped (No.4) (L.D. 2 hrs).

4. Pipe the 3rd line so that the bottom of the 1st and 2nd lines are overpiped (No.4) (L.D. 12 hrs).

5. Remove from waxed paper, turn over and repeat 2.

6. Repeat 3.

7. Repeat 4.

8. Make 6 sugar bells and 12 sugar doves for each tier.

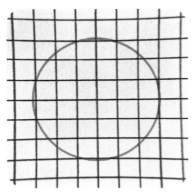

9. Drawing showing template of disc to be cut from paper.

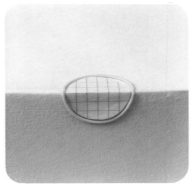

10. Fold disc over top edge of cake and pipe a line around disc top (No.2).

11. Pipe a line around disc on cake side (No.2) (T). Repeat 10–11 on each cake top edge.

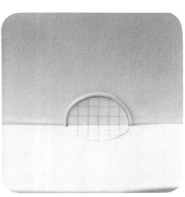

12. Place disc at base of cake and pipe a line around disc on side of cake (No.2) (T).

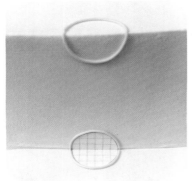

13. Pipe a line around disc on board (No.2). Repeat 12–13 around cake base.

14. Pipe a line beside each No.2 line (No.1).

15. Overpipe each No.2 line (No.1).

16. Pipe an 'S' scroll each side of each cake top pattern, as shown (No.3).

NOTE: *Before attempting to decorate this cake, please study the whole sequence of photographs and notes and ensure you have the proper equipment and materials, as well as sufficient time. Additional information can be found on pages 4-14 and 96.*

17. Pipe curved lines on cake top corners, as shown (No.2).

18. Overpipe each 'S' scroll (No.2).

19. Overpipe each 'S' scroll (No.1).

20. Fix corner decorations.

21. Pipe bulbs each side of each base pattern (No.3).

22. Overpipe the base bulbs with a line (No.2).

23. Overpipe the No.2 line (No.1).

24. Pipe a line each side of each corner decoration, as shown (No.2).

25. Pipe 'L' lines on each cake board corner, as shown (No.2).

26. Pipe a line beside each 'L' line (No.1).

27. Overpipe each board No.2 line (No.1).

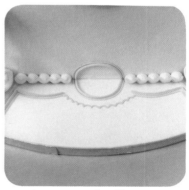

28. Pipe a curve of scallops between each 'L' (No.1).

29. Pipe a curved line beside the scallops (No.1).

30. Fix a bell to each corner decoration.

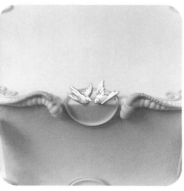

31. Fix doves to each cake top pattern.

32. Fix artificial flowers, fern and ribbon to board, as shown.

Carmen

NOTE: Before attempting to decorate this cake, please study the whole sequence of photographs and notes and ensure you have the proper equipment and materials, as well as sufficient time. Additional information can be found on pages 4-14 and 96.

1. Pipe 10 bulbs of ¼″ diameter and 10 bulbs ⅜″ diameter on waxed paper (No.2) (L.D. 2 hrs).

2. Pipe a series of spikes (using colour of choice) around each bulb (No.1) (L.D. 30m).

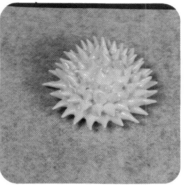

3. Pipe 2 further rows of spikes around each bulb (No.1) (L.D. 30m).

4. Completely enclose each bulb with spikes (No.1) (L.D. 4 hrs).

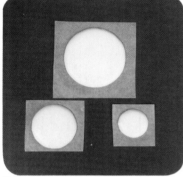

5. Outline and flood-in on waxed paper, 3 discs=one at 1″, one at 1¼″ and one at 2½″. (L.D. 24 hrs).

6. Fix middle sized disc to large disc.

7. Fix the small disc to the middle sized disc.

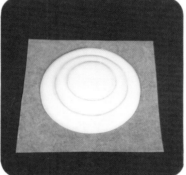

8. Fix flower to small disc.

9. Design for lily petal (height=3¾″) (6 petals required).

10. Using template under waxed paper outline a petal (No.1).

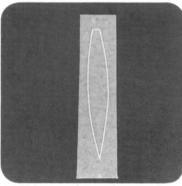

11. Flood-in the petal.

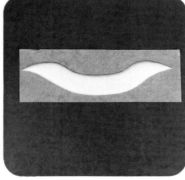

12. Whilst petal is still wet, place on curved piece of tin. Repeat 10, 11 and 12 for each petal. (L.D. 24 hrs).

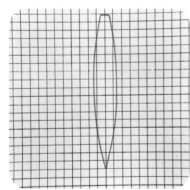

13. Design for cake top runout template (4 required for each cake).

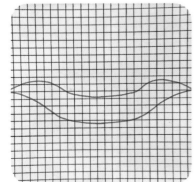

14. Using template under waxed paper, pipe shape outline (No.1).

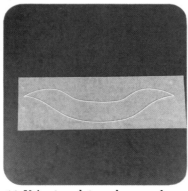

15. Flood-in the runout (L.D. 24 hrs). Repeat 14 and 15 for each shape.

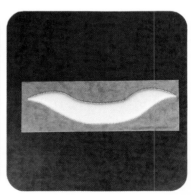

16. Pipe single dots around edge of runouts (No.1) (L.D. 12 hrs).

49

17. Fix and support 1 petal to base of small disc.

18. Repeat 17 on opposite side (L.D. 2 hrs).

19. Fix and support 2 more petals.

20. Fix and support remaining 2 petals (L.D. 12 hrs then remove supports).

21. Fix the 4 runouts around cake top (No.3).

22. Pipe curved line on board following contours of each top runout shape (No.2).

23. Flood-in board between the No.2 line and cake base (L.D. 12 hrs).

24. Pipe plain bulbs on flooded-in areas against cake base (No.3).

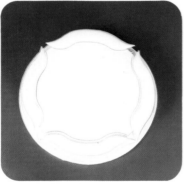

25. Pipe a line along shape of cake-top and board runouts (No.2).

26. Pipe 3 curved lines on cake side under each runout (No.2) (T).

27. Pipe a line beside all the No.2 lines (No.1). (T as necessary).

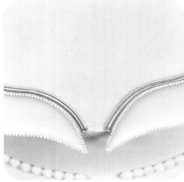

28. Overpipe all No.2 lines (No.1). (T as necessary).

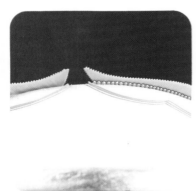

29. Pipe small bulbs under the top runouts (No.2) (T).

30. Pipe tiny bulbs between base of petals and around edge of middle disc (No.1).

31. Fix lily on cake top. Decorate with flowers, artificial leaves and horseshoes.

32. Pipe tiny bulbs around large disc and then pipe coloured spikes at base of each petal (No.1).

NOTE: Before attempting to decorate this cake, please study the whole sequence of photographs and notes and ensure you have the proper equipment and materials, as well as sufficient time. Additional information can be found on pages 4-14 and 96.

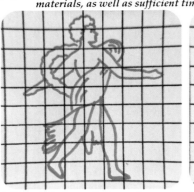

1. Template for male figure (4 figures required).

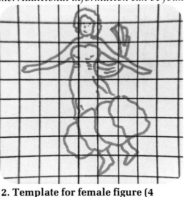

2. Template for female figure (4 figures required).

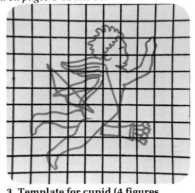

3. Template for cupid (4 figures required).

4. Template for cherub (4 figures required).

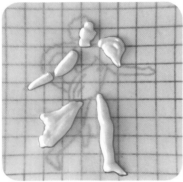

5. Pipe left leg, toga top, face, left arm, and toga back on waxed paper (Template 1) (L.D. 15 m).

6. Pipe hair, garland and toga front (L.D. 15 m).

7. Pipe right leg and back (L.D. 15 m).

8. Pipe right arm and body toga (L.D. 24 hrs).

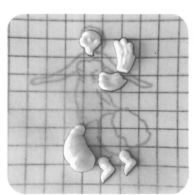

9. Pipe face, feet, flowing waist band and 1st fold of skirt frill on waxed paper (Template 2) (L.D. 15 m).

10. Pipe hair, arms, shoulders and 2nd fold of skirt frill (L.D. 15 m).

11. Pipe bodice, skirt and 3rd fold of skirt frill (L.D. 15 m).

12. Pipe remaining fold of skirt frill (L.D. 24 hrs).

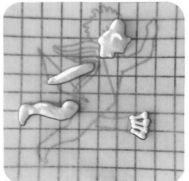

13. Pipe face, left arm, left leg and arrows on waxed paper (Template 3) (L.D. 15 m).

14. Pipe hair, left side of body, quiver and right leg (L.D. 15 m).

15. Pipe right arm, trunk and wing (L.D. 15 m).

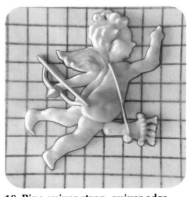

16. Pipe quiver strap, quiver edge and bow (L.D. 24 hrs).

NOTE: *Before attempting to decorate this cake, please study the whole sequence of photographs and notes and ensure you have the proper equipment and materials, as well as sufficient time. Additional information can be found on pages 4-14 and 96.*

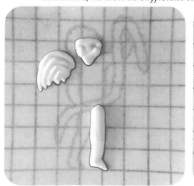

17. Pipe face, wing and left leg on waxed paper (L.D. 15 m).

18. Pipe hair, left arm and right leg. (L.D. 15 m).

19. Pipe trunk and right arm. (L.D. 15 m).

20. Pipe strap and garland. (L.D. 24 hrs).

21. Pipe 4 equally spaced 'V's around cake board (No.2).

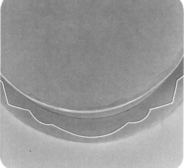

22. Pipe 2 small and 1 large curve between each 'V' (No.2).

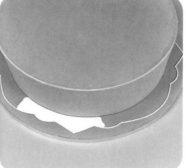

23. Flood-in soft Royal Icing between board line and cake base (L.D. 12 hrs).

24. Pipe large shells around top edge of cake (No.44).

25. Pipe small shells around base of cake (No.43).

26. Pipe a line outside the board runout (No.2).

27. Pipe a line outside the board No.2 line (No.1).

28. Pipe a line on top of the board No.2 line (No.1).

29. Pipe a heart-shape pattern around top edge of cake (No.1).

30. Pipe the floral design shown above each board 'V' on the cake side (No.2) (T).

31. Pipe graduated dots on each side of floral design (No.2).

32. Fix appropriate figures to side of each cake.

Lucille

NOTE: Before attempting to decorate this cake, please study the whole sequence of photographs and notes and ensure you have the proper equipment and materials, as well as sufficient time. Additional information can be found on pages 4–14 and 96.

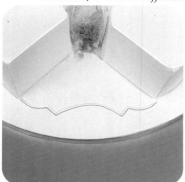

1. Pipe lines on board, as shown, joining the horseshoe ends (No.2).

2. Flood-in the central area of the horseshoe to the outline (L.D. 12 hrs).

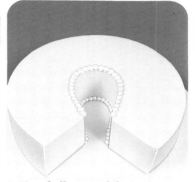

3. Pipe shells around the inside base of the cake (No.42).

4. Pipe shells around the top inner edge (No.42).

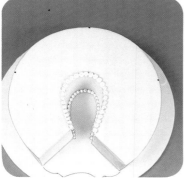

5. Mark outer edge of cake into 4 equal portions with piped dots.

6. Divide each portion into two and mark with piped dots.

7. Pipe 4 curved ropes between each pair of dots (No.42).

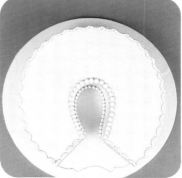

8. Pipe 4 curved ropes along each horseshoe straight edge (No.42).

9. Pipe curved ropes around outside top edge of cake (so they inter-lock inner ropes) (No.42).

10. Mark base of cake with piped dots immediately beneath end of each inner top rope.

11. Pipe a curved rope against bottom side of cake between each pair of dots (No.42) (T).

12. Pipe curved (inter-locking) ropes on the board at base of cake (No.42).

13. Overpipe the top outer ropes with a curved line (No.3).

14. Overpipe the base outer ropes with a curved line (No.3).

15. Pipe curved ropes beside the top shells (No.2).

16. Pipe a curved line beside each inner top rope (No.2).

17. Overpipe the top inner ropes (No.2).

18. Overpipe the top outer No.3 line (No.2).

19. Pipe a curved line under each top outer rope (No.2) (T).

20. Pipe a rope against each cake base rope (No.2) (T).

21. Overpipe the No.3 board line (No.2).

22. Outline the base design (No.2).

23. Pipe a line beside the cake top No.2 line (No.1).

24. Overpipe the top No.2 line (No.1).

25. Overpipe the top inner rope (No.1).

26. Overpipe the outer No.2 line (No.1).

27. Pipe a line under cake-side No.2 line and then against the No.2 line (No.1) (T).

28. Pipe curved ropes against the base ropes (No.1) (T).

29. Overpipe the board rope line (No.1).

30. Pipe a line beside the No.2 board line and then overpipe the No.2 line (No.1).

31. Pipe 2 graduated dots between each top shell and then overpipe top outer No.1 line (No.1).

32. Pipe lines, as shown, to entrance and around cake base (No.1). Fix ribbon to board edge.

56

1. Cut a piece of paper the same size as cake-top.

2. Fold paper in half.

3. Fold paper in half again.

4. Fold paper in half again.

5. Draw a curve on the paper, as shown.

6. Cut-off the portion shown.

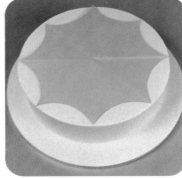

7. Open paper template and place on cake-top.

8. Pipe curved lines beside the template (No. 3) then remove template.

9. Pipe curved lines on cake-board, as shown (No.3).

10. Pipe a line inside each No.3 cake-top curved line (No.2).

11. Overpipe each No.3 cake-top line (No.2).

12. Pipe a line beside each cake-board No.3 line (No.2).

13. Overpipe each cake-board No.3 line (No.2).

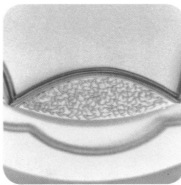

14. Filigree inside each cake-top curve, as shown (No.1).

15. Filigree inside each cake-board curve, as shown (No.1).

16. Pipe a line inside each cake-top No.2 line (No.1).

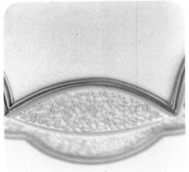

17. Overpipe each cake-top central line (No. 1).

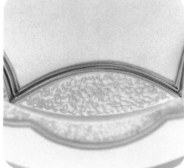

18. Overpipe each outer cake-top No.2 line (No.1).

19. Pipe a line beside each cake-board No.2 line (No.1).

20. Overpipe each cake-board central line (No.1).

21. Overpipe each cake-board inner line (No.1).

22. Pipe bulbs along cake-top edge (No.4).

23. Pipe bulbs along cake-base (No.4).

24. Overpipe each cake-top bulb with smaller bulb (No.3).

25. Overpipe each cake-base bulb with smaller bulb (No.3).

26. Pipe a loop linking each cake-top pair of bulbs (No.2).

27. Pipe a loop linking each cake-base pair of bulbs (No.2).

28. Fix ribbon around cake-side, as shown.

29. Fix ribbon to form bow, as shown.

30. Fix loop of ribbon to form bow knot.

31. Fix flowers of choice to centre of alternate cake-top curves.

32. Pipe a leaf each side of each flower (leaf bag).

Lisa

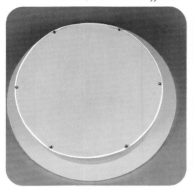

1. Mark top of cake with small piped dots into 6 equal spaces (No.1).

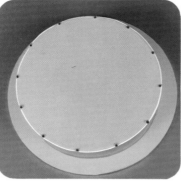

2. Now mark top of cake into 12 equal spaces (No.1).

3. Pipe a line around base of cake (No.44).

4. Immediately beneath each top dot, mark line around base with a piped dot (No.1).

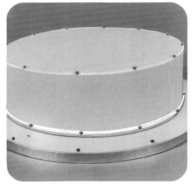

5. Immediately opposite each base dot mark board edge with a piped dot (No.1).

6. Pipe 'S' scroll from left to right between 2 dots on top edge (No.44).

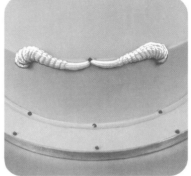

7. Pipe 'S' scroll from right to left between 2 dots on top edge (No.44).

8. Pipe 'C' scroll from left to right inside 'S' scroll (No.44).

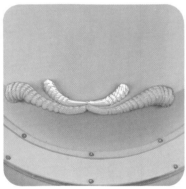

9. Pipe 'C' scroll from right to left inside 'S' scroll (No.44).

10. Repeat scroll designs around top edge of cake.

11. Pipe 'S' scroll between 2 dots on the No.44 line (directly beneath a matching top scroll) (No.44).

12. Pipe 'S' scroll between 2 dots on the No.44 line (directly beneath the next matching top scroll) (No.44).

13. Repeat scroll design around base of cake.

14. Overpipe a top left-to-right 'S' scroll (No.3).

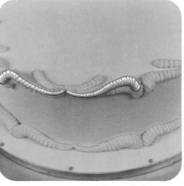

15. Overpipe a top right-to-left 'S' scroll (No.3).

16. Overpipe a top left-to-right 'C' scroll (No.3).

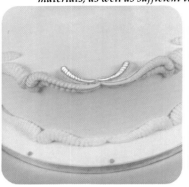

17. Overpipe a top right-to-left 'C' scroll (No.3). Repeat 14–17 around cake top.

18. Overpipe base scrolls (No.3).

19. Practice flower motif in numerical order (No.3).

20. Pipe flower motif inside each top 'C' scroll (No.3).

21. Overpipe a top left-to-right 'S' scroll (No.2).

22. Overpipe the next top right-to-left 'S' scroll (No.2).

23. Overpipe a top left-to-right 'C' scroll (No.2).

24. Overpipe the next top right-to-left 'C' scroll (No.2). Repeat 21–24 around cake top.

25. Overpipe base scrolls (No.2).

26. Pipe 3 curved lines below scrolls on side of cake (No.2). (T). Continue around cake.

27. Pipe line pattern on board (No.2). Continue around cake and remove marker dots.

28. Pipe line around cake under 1st line (No.1) (T).

29. Pipe a line on board in front of 1st line (No.1).

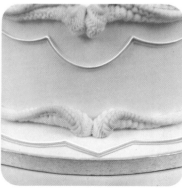

30. Pipe a line against 1st line around side of cake (T) and on 1st board line (No.1).

31. Overpipe each scroll (No.1). Pipe scallops on side of cake and on board (No.1) (T).

32. Form a central motif with artificial flowers and decorative piping (No.1).

62

  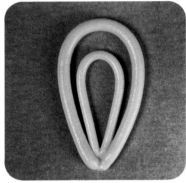 

1. Pipe first sweet-pea petal, as shown, on waxed paper (No.57).

2. Pipe second petal, as shown (No.57).

3. Pipe sweet-pea centre (No.57).

4. Pipe calyx, as shown (No.2).

 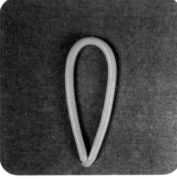 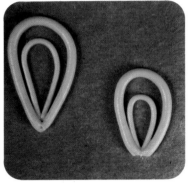 (7 etc.)

5. Pipe 250 assorted sweet-peas (L.D. 24 hrs).

6. Pipe a loop shape on waxed paper (No.2).

7. Pipe an inner loop (No.1).

8. Pipe 80 assorted double loops and 12 love-birds (L.D. 24 hrs).

9. Cut two strips of paper to form cross and place on cake-top, as shown.

10. Pipe a line beside the cross (No.4). Remove paper cross.

11. Continue piping lines down cake-sides (No.4) (T).

12. Continue piping lines across cake-board (No.4).

13. Pipe a line beside each No.4 line (No.3) and then over-pipe each No.4 line (No.3) (T as necessary).

14. Pipe a line beside each No.3 line (No.2) and then over-pipe each No.3 line (No.2) (T as necessary).

15. Pipe a line beside each No.2 line (No.1) and then over-pipe each No.2 line (No.1) (T as necessary).

16. Pipe shells around cake-base corners (No.3).

17. Pipe curved lines at each cake-base corner (No.2).

18. Pipe curved line at each cake-base corner, as shown (No.2).

19. Pipe shells around each cake-board outer edge corner (No.2).

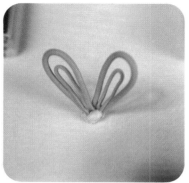

20. Fix loops to cake-top centre, as shown.

21. Fix two further loops to complete cake-top centre decoration.

22. Fix loop and sweet-pea to a cake-top corner.

23. Fix further sweet-peas, as shown.

24. Fix further loops, as shown.

25. Fix further sweet-peas and loops, as shown.

26. Fix further sweet-peas and loops, as shown.

27. Fix further sweet-peas and loops, as shown.

28. Fix further sweet-peas and loops, as shown.

29. Picture showing completed corner. Repeat 22–28 at each cake corner.

30. Fix a love-bird to each cake-top central panel.

31. Fix artificial horseshoe to base of each central panel.

32. Fix matching velvet ribbon to cake-board.

Anne

66

NOTE: Before attempting to decorate this cake, please study the whole sequence of photographs and notes and ensure you have the proper equipment and materials, as well as sufficient time. Additional information can be found on pages 4-14 and 96.

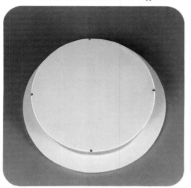

1. Mark top of cake into 4 equal spaces with small dots (No.1).

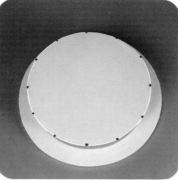

2. Now mark each quarter of cake-top into 3 equal spaces (dividing top edge into 12) (No.1).

3. Now halve and mark each division (creating 24 divisions in all) (No.1).

4. Repeat on base of cake, keeping marks immediately beneath the top marks (No.1).

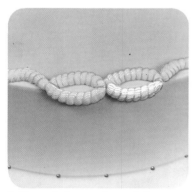

5. Pipe a curved rope between 2 dots (No.43).

6. Pipe a 2nd curved rope between dots (No.43).

7. Continue piping *uniform* curved ropes around top of cake (No.43).

8. Pipe a curved rope against the side of the cake, linking ends with previous curves (No.43).

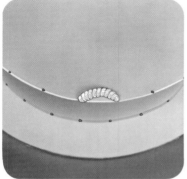

9. Pipe a 2nd curved rope between dots (No.43).

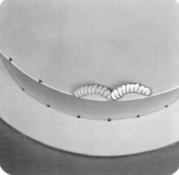

10. Continue piping *uniform* curved ropes around side of cake (No.43).

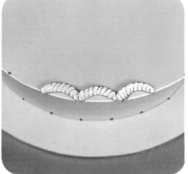

11. Pipe a spiral shell between 2 dots on base (No.43).

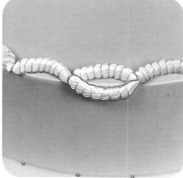

12. Pipe 2nd spiral shell between dots on base (No.43).

13. Continue piping *uniform* spiral shells around base of cake (No.43).

14. Overpipe a top rope (No.3).

15. Overpipe the next top rope (No.3).

16. Continue *uniform* overpiping of top ropes (No.3).

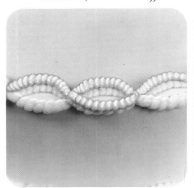

17. Overpipe a rope on side of cake (No.3).

18. Overpipe the next rope (No.3).

19. Continue overpiping the side ropes (No.3).

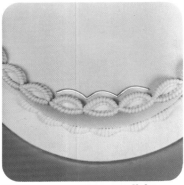

20. Pipe a curved line parallel to ropes on top of cake (No.2).

21. Pipe a curved line under each rope around side of cake (No.2) (T).

22. Pipe a curved line parallel to each spiral shell on board (No.2).

23. Overpipe the top ropes (No.2).

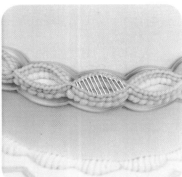

24. Overpipe the side ropes (No.2).

25. Pipe a line inside the No.2 line on cake top and then overpipe the No.2 line (No.1).

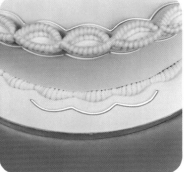

26. Pipe a line on board outside the No.2 line and then overpipe the No.2 line (No.1).

27. Pipe a line under the No.2 line on cake side and then pipe a line against the No.2 line (No.1) (T).

28. Pipe diagonal lines – from left to right – across rope pattern with coloured icing (No.1). (Repeat around cake).

29. Overpipe diagonal lines – from right to left – on rope pattern with coloured icing (No.1). (Repeat around cake).

30. Overpipe lattice ends with plain shells (No.2).

31. Fix hand-made rosebuds and artificial leaves at 4 equally spaced points around base of cake.

32. Fix top decoration of hand-made rosebuds and roses. (See instructions for making flowers).

1. Mark cake-top edge into 20 equal spaces with small piped dots.

2. Pipe a curved rope between two marker dots (No.43).

3. Continue piping ropes between dots, as shown (No.43).

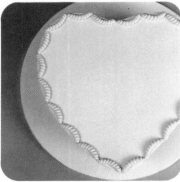

4. Continue piping ropes between dots, as shown (No.43).

5. Pipe a joining curved rope between two dots on cake-side (No.43) (T).

6. Continue piping curved ropes around cake side, as shown (No.43) (T).

7. Pipe curved ropes around cake-base, as shown (No.43) (T).

8. Pipe curved ropes around cake-board, as shown (No.43).

9. Pipe a bulb between each pair of cake-top ropes (No.3).

10. Pipe graduated bulbs each side of each central bulb (No.2).

11. Repeat 9 and 10 at cake-base.

12. Overpipe each cake-top inner rope (No.3).

13. Overpipe each cake-side rope (No.3).

14. Overpipe each cake-base rope (No.3) (T).

15. Overpipe each cake-board rope (No.3).

16. Pipe a line beside each cake-top rope (No.2).

17. Pipe a straight line from each cake-top join (No.2).

18. Pipe a line beneath each cake-side curved rope (No.2) (T).

19. Pipe a straight line from each cake-side join (No.2) (T).

20. Repeat 18 and 19 at cake-base.

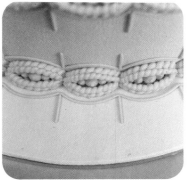

21. Repeat 18 and 19 on cake-board.

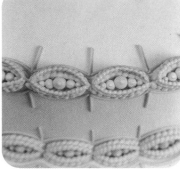

22. Overpipe each cake-top and cake-side rope (No.2).

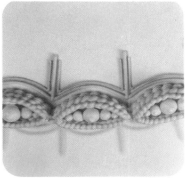

23. Overpipe each cake-base and cake-board rope (No.2) (T as necessary).

24. Pipe a line beside each cake-top No.2 line (No.1).

25. Overpipe each cake-top No.2 line (No.1).

26. Repeat 24 and 25 at cake-side and on cake-board, as shown.

27. Overpipe each cake-top and cake-side rope (No.1).

28. Overpipe each cake-base and cake-board rope (No.1) (T as necessary).

29. Pipe the part of the bow shown on cake-side (No.1) (T).

30. Complete the bow, as shown (No.1) (T).

31. Pipe curved lines around cake-board edge (No.1).

32. Pipe a bulb at each curve (No.1).

Heather

1. Pipe 4 dots at points on diagonal line (corner to corner).

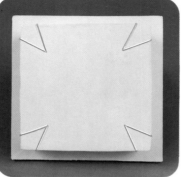

2. Pipe straight lines from dots to edge of cake (No.2).

3. Continue lines down side of cake (No.2) (T).

4. Continue lines to corner of board (No.2). Repeat at each corner.

5. Pipe a line beside each cake-top No.2 line (No.1).

6. Pipe a line beside each cake-side No.2 line (No.1).

7. Pipe a line beside each board No.2 line (No.1).

8. Overpipe each cake-top No.2 line (No.1).

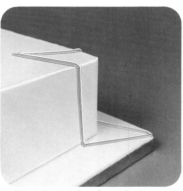

9. Overpipe each cake-side No.2 line (No.1).

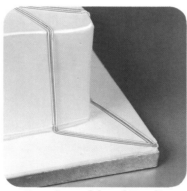

10. Overpipe each board No.2 line (No.1).

11. Pipe scallops beside the lines on each corner (No.1).

12. Filigree each corner (No.1).

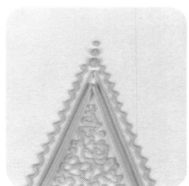

13. Pipe 3 graduated dots on top of cake to complete each corner design (No.1).

14. Pipe plain shells along top edges of cake (No.4).

15. Pipe plain shells around base of cake (No.4).

16. Overpipe top and base shells (No.3).

17. Pipe 2 equal curves between each corner design (No.2).

18. Repeat curves against each side of cake (No.2) (T).

19. Repeat curves on cake board (No.2).

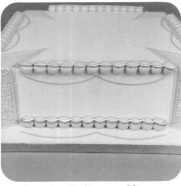

20. Overpipe both top and base shells (No.2).

21. Pipe a line beside the top curved line (No.1).

22. Pipe a line under side curved line (No.1) (T).

23. Pipe a line beside the base curved line (No.1).

24. Overpipe 1st curved line on cake top (No.1).

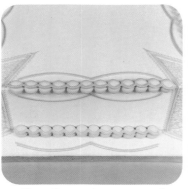

25. Pipe a line against 1st curved line on side of cake (No.1) (T).

26. Overpipe 1st curved line on base (No.1).

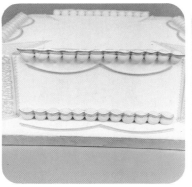

27. Overpipe top and base shells with coloured Royal Icing (No.1).

28. Curve 4 artificial silver leaves and fix centrally.

29. Using artificial flower of choice, fix to centre of leaves.

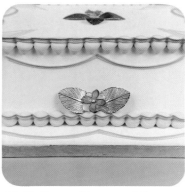

30. Fix 2 curved leaves and flower on centre of each side.

31. Fix silver shoe (or other motif of choice) with matching flowers to each corner.

32. Finish top corners with hand-made sugar doves.

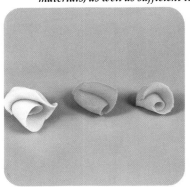

1. 80–100 rose-buds need to be made for each tier – see instructions.

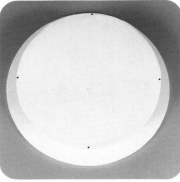

2. Mark top of cake into 4 equal divisions with piped dots.

3. Pipe a curved line, as shown, between each dot (No.2).

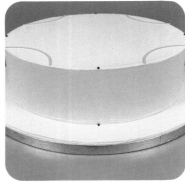

4. Mark base of cake (beneath top dots) into 4 equal divisions with piped dots.

5. Pipe curved line on cake board around each base dot, as shown (No.2).

6. Pipe a line inside each No.2 top line and outside each No.2 board line (No.1).

7. Overpipe all No.2 lines (No.1).

8. Pipe plain shells inside all No.2 lines and on parts of the cake edge shown (No.2).

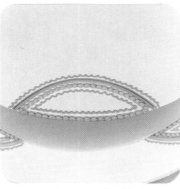

9. Pipe scallops outside all No.1 lines (No.1) and then inside all shells (No.1).

10. Pipe 4 spiral shells on top edge between each design (No.43).

11. Repeat 10 on cake board (No.43).

12. Overpipe all spiral shells with a rope (No.3).

13. Pipe a curved rope inside cake-top spiral shells (No.2).

14. Pipe a curved rope beneath cake-top spiral shells (No.2) (T).

15. Pipe a curved rope over base spiral shells (No.2) (T).

16. Pipe a curved rope on board around base spiral shells (No.2).

76

17. Overpipe all top spiral shell ropes (No.2).

18. Overpipe all base spiral shell ropes (No.2).

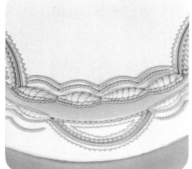

19. Pipe a line inside each cake top No.2 rope (No.2).

20. Pipe a line on the cake side under each top rope (No.2) (T).

21. Pipe a line over each base No.2 rope (No.2) (T) and then pipe a line outside each board No.2 rope (No.2).

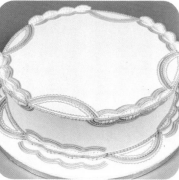

22. Pipe a line beside each No.2 line (No.1) (T as necessary).

23. Overpipe each No.2 line (No.1) and then pipe a line against each No.2 line (No.1) (T as necessary).

24. Overpipe all top and base spiral shell ropes (No.1).

25. Pipe 2 bird heads on cake side, as shown, under the 1st pair of spiral shells (No.1).

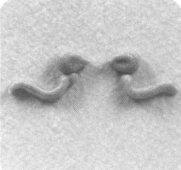

26. Pipe bird bodies (No.1).

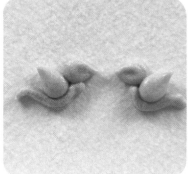

27. Pipe bird wings (No.1).

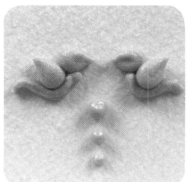

28. Pipe 3 graduated dots beneath each bird (No.1).

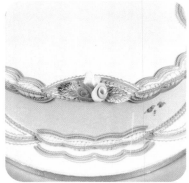

29. Fix 3 sugar rose-buds and artificial leaves as shown.

30. Fix, as shown, further rose-buds down cake side.

31. Finish spray with smaller rose-buds and artificial leaves.

32. Pipe leaves with leaf shaped piping bag. Repeat 29–32 three more times around cake.

Dulcie

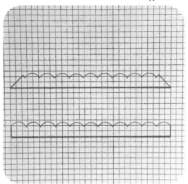

1. Drawing showing template of cake-top and cake-side runouts.

2. Drawing showing template of heart and bell runouts.

3. Outline and flood-in 6 cake-top runouts on waxed paper (L.D. 24 hrs).

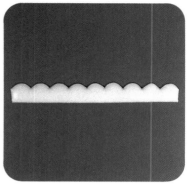

4. Outline and flood-in 12 cake-side runouts on waxed paper (L.D. 24 hrs).

5. Outline and flood-in 3 pairs of bell runouts on waxed paper (L.D. 1 hr).

6. Outline and flood-in 3 pairs of heart runouts on waxed paper (L.D. 24 hrs).

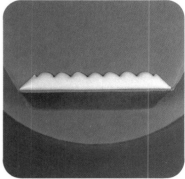

7. Pipe a bulb to each bell (No. 1) (L.D. 24 hrs).

8. Fix a cake-top runout in the position shown.

9. Fix remaining cake-top runouts, as shown.

10. Fix a cake-side runout in the position shown.

11. Fix remaining cake-side top runouts and then fix a cake-side base runout, as shown.

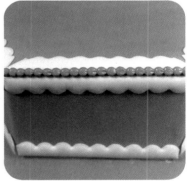

12. Fix remaining cake-side base runouts and then pipe shells around cake-top edge (No. 2).

13. Pipe shells around cake-base (No. 2).

14. Picture showing cake so far.

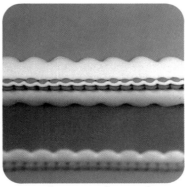

15. Pipe a line over cake-top edge shells (No. 2).

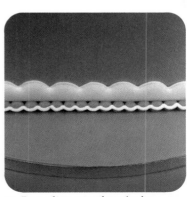

16. Pipe a line over the cake-base shells (No. 2).

79

17. Overpipe each No. 2 line (No. 1).

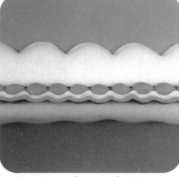

18. Overpipe cake-top edge No. 1 line (No. 1).

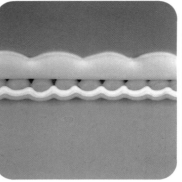

19. Overpipe cake-base No. 1 line (No. 1).

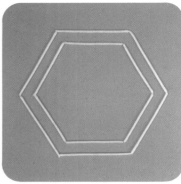

20. Pipe two hexagonals on cake-top centre (No. 1).

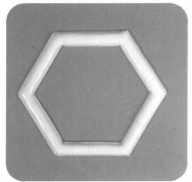

21. Flood-in between the hexagonal lines (L.D. 1 hr).

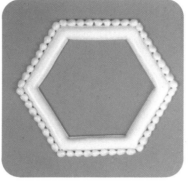

22. Pipe shells around the hexagon (No. 1).

23. Pipe a line on the hexagon, as shown (No. 2) and then overpipe the No. 2 line (No. 1).

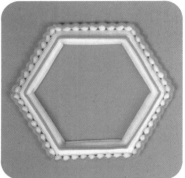

24. Pipe a line over the hexagon shells (No. 1).

25. Pipe curved lines around cake-board edge (No. 1).

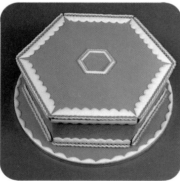

26. Flood-in the cake-board edge curves (L.D. 1 hr).

27. Pipe shells around cake-board edge (No. 2).

28. Pipe a line over the cake-board edge shells (No. 1).

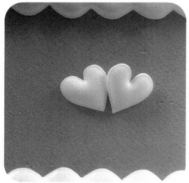

29. Fix a pair of hearts to alternate cake sides.

30. Fix a pair of bells to alternate sides and then pipe a bulb at the top of each pair (No. 1).

31. Fix decorations of choice to each point, as shown.

32. Fix matching decorations to cake-top centre.

1. Mark cake-top edge into six equal spaces with small piped dots.

2. Join each dot with a piped curved line (No. 3).

3. Repeat 1 on cake-base and then join each dot with a curved line, as shown (No. 3).

4. Pipe 'C's at each cake-top join, as shown (No. 42).

5. Pipe 'S' scroll from left to right at each cake-top join (No. 42).

6. Pipe 'S' scroll from right to left at each cake-top join (No. 42).

7. Pipe 'S' scroll from left to right at each cake-top join (No. 42) (T).

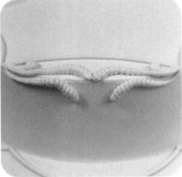

8. Pipe 'S' Scroll from right to left at each cake-top join (No. 42) (T).

9. Pipe a line inside each cake-board curved line, around cake-base (No. 42).

10. Pipe a left-hand scroll at each cake-base join (No. 42).

11. Pipe a right-hand scroll at each cake-base join (No. 42).

12. Pipe a line inside each cake-top No. 3 line (No. 2).

13. Overpipe each cake-top No. 3 line (No. 2).

14. Pipe a line over each left-hand 'C' (No. 2).

15. Pipe a line over each right-hand 'C' (No. 2).

16. Overpipe each cake-top left-hand scroll (No. 2).

NOTE: Before attempting to decorate this cake, please study the whole sequence of photographs and notes and ensure you have the proper equipment and materials, as well as sufficient time. Additional information can be found on pages 4-14 and 96.

17. Overpipe each cake-top right-hand scroll (No. 2).

18. Overpipe each cake-side left-hand scroll (No. 2) (T).

19. Overpipe each cake-side right-hand scroll (No. 2) (T).

20. Overpipe each cake-base scroll (No. 2).

21. Picture showing stage reached.

22. Pipe a line beside each cake-board No. 3 line (No. 2).

23. Overpipe each cake-board No. 3 line (No. 2).

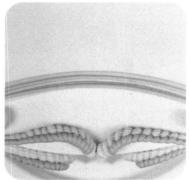

24. Pipe a line beside each cake-top No. 2 line (No. 1).

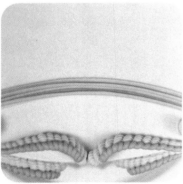

25. Overpipe each cake-top No. 2 line (No. 1).

26. Overpipe each cake-top and cake-side scroll (No. 1) (T as necessary).

27. Overpipe each cake-board scroll (No. 1).

28. Pipe a line beside each cake-board No. 2 line (No. 1) and then overpipe each No. 2 line (No. 1).

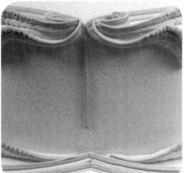

29. Pipe a vertical line on cake-side (below each join) (No. 2) (T).

30. Pipe a line each side of each vertical No. 2 line then overpipe each No. 2 line (No. 1) (T).

31. Fix artificial decorations of choice to cake-top centre.

32. Fix rose, as shown.

83

Frances

NOTE: Before attempting to decorate this cake, please study the whole sequence of photographs and notes and ensure you have the proper equipment and materials, as well as sufficient time. Additional information can be found on pages 4–14 and 96.

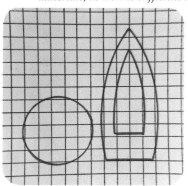

1. Drawing showing template of cake-centre design and base runouts.

2. Outline and flood-in on waxed paper the cake-centre runout.

3. Immediately place in curved position, as shown (L.D. 24 hrs) (4 required).

4. Outline and flood-in on waxed paper the base runout (L.D. 24 hrs).

5. Pipe assorted roses, as shown, on waxed paper (Various petal tubes) (L.D. 24 hrs).

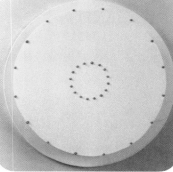

6. Divide cake-top edge and centre into 16 equal portions with piped dots.

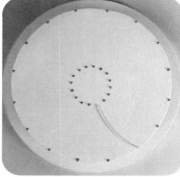

7. Pipe a curved line from a central dot to an outer dot, as shown (No.3).

8. Pipe the lines shown to complete pattern (No.3).

9. Repeat 7 and 8 to form uniform pattern, as shown. Remove remaining dots.

10. Divide cake-base and board into 16 equal portions with piped dots, as shown.

11. Pipe joining cuved line on cake-side, as shown (No.3) (T).

12. Pipe further curved line on cake-side, as shown (No.3) (T) (Repeat 11 and 12 around cake).

13. Pipe joining curved lines on cake-board, as shown (No.3) (Repeat around cake-board). Remove remaining dots.

14. Pipe a line outside each No.3 line (No.2) (T as necessary).

15. Overpipe each No.3 line (No.2) (T as necessary).

16. Pipe a line outside each No.2 line (No.1) (T as necessary).

17. Overpipe each No.2 line (No.1) (T as necessary).

18. Pipe a scalloped line outside each No.1 line (No.1) (T as necessary).

19. Filigree inside each pattern (No.1).

20. Pipe shells around cake-top edge between each pattern (No.43).

21. Pipe shells around cake-base between each pattern (No.43).

22. Pipe filigree in each central runout design (No.0) (L.D. 2 hrs).

23. Pipe shells around base runout (No.1) (L.D. 2 hrs).

24. Fix two leaf designs in position shown and support with pillars (L.D. 2 hrs).

25. Fix remaining two leaf designs, as shown and support with pillars (L.D. 2 hrs).

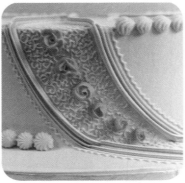

26. Flood-in the central area shown (L.D. 24 hrs).

27. Fix assorted roses on each cake-side panel, as shown.

28. Pipe leaves, as shown (Leaf bag) (T).

29. Fix roses and a horseshoe between each cake-side panel, then pipe leaves, as shown (Leaf bag).

30. Fix horseshoe to centre of cake-top design.

31. Fix roses to base of horseshoe, as shown.

32. Pipe leaves, as shown (Leaf bag).

1. Mark the top of a square cake with 4 dots (in the positions shown).

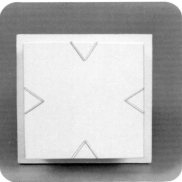

2. Pipe lines from each dot to form triangles at cake top edges (No.2).

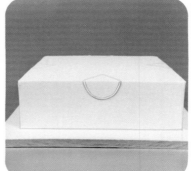

3. Pipe a curved line on each side of the cake to meet the top triangular lines (No.2) (T).

4. Pipe a 'V' centrally on cake board. Repeat on each side (No.2).

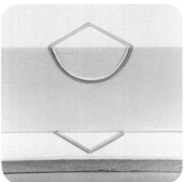

5. Pipe a line beside each No.2 line (No.1) (T as necessary).

6. Overpipe all No.2 lines (No.1) and then pipe a line against each No.2 line (No.1) (T as necessary).

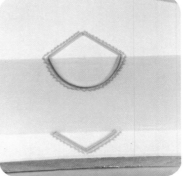

7. Pipe scallops around all the No.1 lines (No.1) (T as necessary).

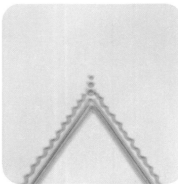

8. Pipe 3 graduated dots at each cake top triangular point (No.1).

9. Filigree each pattern (No.1).

10. Pipe a line around each base corner to meet each 'V' (No.44).

11. Pipe an 'S' scroll from left to right on cake top edge (No.44).

12. Pipe an 'S' scroll from right to left on cake top edge (No.44).

13. Pipe a 'C' scroll inside each 'S' scroll (No.44).

14. Repeat 11–13 around cake top edge.

15. Pipe an 'S' scroll at each cake base corner (No.44).

16. Overpipe each cake top 'S' scroll (No.3).

17. Overpipe each cake top 'C' scroll (No.3).

18. Overpipe each cake base 'S' scroll (No.3).

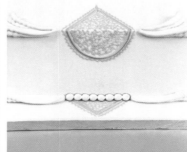

19. Pipe plain shells between 'S' scrolls at cake base (No.3).

20. Overpipe each 'S' scroll on cake top (No.2).

21. Overpipe each 'C' scroll on cake top (No.2).

22. Overpipe each 'S' scroll at cake base (No.2).

23. Pipe 2 curved lines on cake side under each top 'S' scroll (No.2)(T).

24. Pipe 2 curved lines and a 'V' at each cake board corner (No.2).

25. Pipe a line under each cake side No.2 line and then against each cake side No.2 line (No.1)(T).

26. Pipe a line beside each cake board No.2 line (No.1) and then overpipe each cake board No.2 line (No.1).

27. Pipe lines from the 'C' to the 'S' scrolls on cake top (No.1).

28. Overpipe cross lines with curved ones (to form latticework) and then overpipe each scroll (No.1)

29. Pipe a curved line above each base scroll (No.1) and then pipe lines from each curved line to each scroll (No.1).

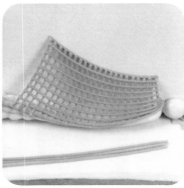

30. Overpipe the cross lines with curved ones (to form latticework) (No.1).

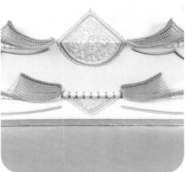

31. Pipe shells along each curved line and then overpipe each base scroll. Overpipe the shells with a line (all No.1).

32. Fix artificial flowers and decorations of choice at triangle centres and cake base corners.

Amelia

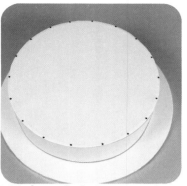

1. Mark top of cake into 18 equal spaces with small dots.

2. Pipe a line around the cake base (No.43).

3. Mark the No.43 line into 18 equal spaces immediately beneath the top dots.

4. Pipe a scroll measuring ²⁄₃rds the distance between 2 dots on top edge of cake (No.43).

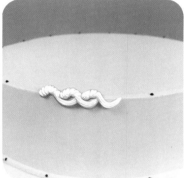

5. Continue scrolls around top edge of cake so there are 3 scroll heads between dots (No.43).

6. Repeat 4 on base line (No.43).

7. Repeat 5 (No.43).

8. Overpipe a top scroll (No.3).

9. Continue overpiping all top scrolls (No.3).

10. Overpipe a base scroll with another scroll (No.3).

11. Continue overpiping all base scrolls (No.3).

12. Overpipe a top scroll with another scroll (No.2).

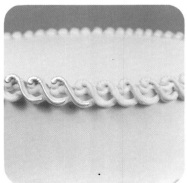

13. Continue overpiping all top scrolls (No.2).

14. Overpipe a base scroll with another scroll (No.2).

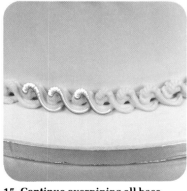

15. Continue overpiping all base scrolls (No.2).

16. Overpipe a top scroll with another scroll (No.1).

17. Continue overpiping all top scrolls (No.1).

18. Overpipe a base scroll with another scroll (No.1).

19. Continue overpiping all base scrolls (No.1).

20. Place a cake board on cake top and mark out 18 spaces with small dots.

21. Remove cake board and pipe a curved line between each dot (No.2).

22. Pipe curved lines on side of cake beneath and symmetrical with top curved lines (No.2) (T).

23. Pipe curved lines above base scrolls to match the curved lines in 22 (No.2) (T).

24. Pipe curved lines on cake board to match other curved lines (No.2).

25. Pipe a line outside the No.2 line on cake top (No.1).

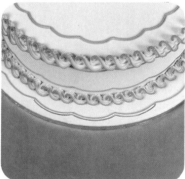

26. Pipe a line outside the No.2 line on cake board (No.1).

27. Pipe flower stem on cake side (No.2) (T).

28. Pipe second stem (No.2) (T). Repeat 27 and 28 around cake side.

29. Practise piping lily of the valley shape before piping directly to cake (No.1).

30. Pipe lilies of the valley around side of cake (No.1) (T).

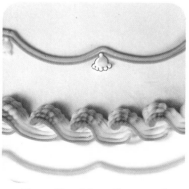

31. Pipe a lily of the valley at each curve point on cake top (No.1).

32. Make 3 sugar bells (see instructions) and fix on top centre of cake. Pipe 3 short lines (No.1).

Teresa

NOTE: *Before attempting to decorate this cake, please study the whole sequence of photographs and notes and ensure you have the proper equipment and materials, as well as sufficient time. Additional information can be found on pages 4-14 and 96.*

1. Pipe a line around cake-top, as shown (No.3).

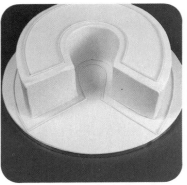

2. Pipe a line around cake-board, as shown (No.3).

3. Filigree between the No.3 line and cake-top edge (No.1).

4. Filigree between the No.3 line and cake-base (No.1).

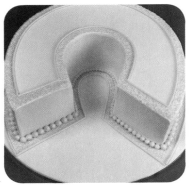

5. Pipe bulbs around inside of horseshoe (No.2) and then around remainder of cake-base (No.3).

6. Pipe bulbs around the part of the cake-top edge shown (No.2).

7. Pipe a 'C' scroll from right to left on each cake-top front edge, as shown (No.3).

8. Pipe a 'C' scroll from left to right on each cake-top front edge, as shown (No.3).

9. Pipe a 'C' line on the cake-top corner shown (No.3).

10. Pipe two further 'C' scrolls on the cake-top edge shown (No.3).

11. Repeat 9 and 10 in opposite direction on opposite cake-top edge.

12. Pipe bulbs around remainder of cake-top edge (No.3).

13. Pipe a line inside the cake-top No.3 line (No.2).

14. Pipe a line outside the cake-board No.3 line (No.2).

15. Overpipe the cake-top No.3 line (No.2).

16. Overpipe each cake-top scroll and 'C' line (No.2).

94

17. Pipe an 'S' line over two cake-top No.3 bulbs, as shown (No.2).

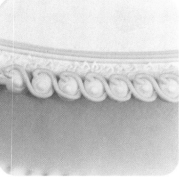

18. Continue piping 'S' lines over cake-top No.3 bulbs (No.2).

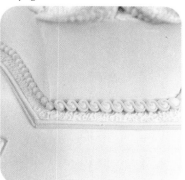

19. Pipe 'S' lines over cake-base No.3 bulbs (No.2).

20. Pipe two curved lines at each cake-side end (No.2) (T).

21. Overpipe the cake-board No.3 line (No.2).

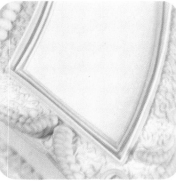

22. Pipe a line inside the cake-top No.2 line (No.1) and then over-pipe each No.2 line (No.1).

23. Overpipe each cake-top scroll and 'C' line (No.1).

24. Overpipe each 'S' line (No.1).

25. Pipe a line outside the cake-board No.2 line (No.1) and then overpipe each No.2 line (No.1).

26. Pipe a line beneath each cake-side No.2 line (No.1) and then overpipe each No.2 line (No.1) (T).

27. Pipe initials of choice on each cake-side end (No.2) (T).

28. Pipe a line beside each initial (No.1) and then overpipe each No.2 line (No.1) (T).

29. Pipe shells against initials, as shown (No.1) (T).

30. Pipe curved lines on cake-board (No.2) and then filigree in area shown (No.1).

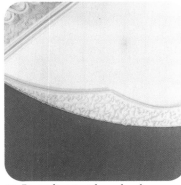

31. Pipe a line inside each cake-board No.2 curved line (No.1) and then overpipe each No. 2 line (No.1).

32. Fix decorations of choice.

Index/Glossary.